CITY PROPHET

PREPARING THE PEOPLE FOR THE COMING OF THE LORD

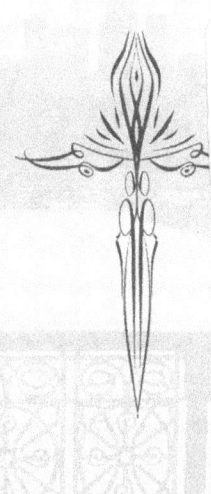

A PARABLE OF ENLIGHTENMENT AND REVOLUTION

DANIEL ORR

First published by Busybird Publishing 2024

Copyright © 2024 Daniel Orr

ISBN:
Paperback: 978-0-646-89229-0
Ebook: 978-0-646-89815-5

This book is copyright. Apart from any fair dealing for the purposes of study, research, criticism, review, or as otherwise permitted under the Copyright Act, no part may be reproduced by any process without written permission. Enquiries should be made through the publisher.

This is a work of fiction. Any similarities between places and characters are a coincidence.

Cover design: Busybird Publishing

Layout and typesetting: Busybird Publishing

Editor: Skye Blake

Busybird Publishing
2/118 Para Road
Montmorency, Victoria
Australia 3094
www.busybird.com.au

MISSION STATEMENT

What began as a story of one, Zenith, and his mirror soul, Armi, a mystic union long cast away from the world, returns to it, in brief, to share the knowingness and wisdom of Self, has also unwittingly prepared the people for God's own light, in all His Son's manliness.

The message and example of *City Prophet* reveals the divinity of God expressed as the Lord of enlightenment manifest. Thus, the resulting inheritance of this work, as support everlasting, is owed to the truth of the Lord's coming.

The purpose of the book is to inspire and empower the reader to become Self and God realized, through parable and poem. To embody that consciousness through such story and spirit, breathes the Lord's fire and draws from soul right down to the marrow. Embodiment makes transfiguration of enlightenment a way of life and is central to the author's aim herein.

Pivotal to the book's legacy is the author's ability to detail the critical gates and classical confrontations within the kingdom of God. This was certainly the most challenging aspect of the 22-year writing process with some of the latter poems only manifesting from 2014-15 onwards. Prior to that, there was no ability to explain in poetic form the initial experience of enlightenment, (age 27 in 2001) irrespective of the herculean effort to do so.

In succeeding, the book offers a reference and guide to navigating the enlightened conditions of God's kingdom and provides a compass to track one's awareness all the way to God's own view. Passing the timeless void/wilderness, the evolution proceeds onwards to becoming one with the 'all' that is. Via the source of 'all' as God, reveals Christ the Son of God *and* man upon the clouds of Heaven in the greatest glory now and always. It's a sovereign rise after the fall crowned on top of the world, where Light is unmoved above and below, shining its radiance within and without.

A NOTE TO THE READER

In essence, the evolution of Zenith, and thus revolution of divinity, inspires and confronts in equal measure. The work herein has been written in such a way as to transport the reader all the way beyond, and for the reader in turn to take it wherever they deem necessary. If moved to, you are encouraged to delve deeper into the teachings of the parable and create something new from it: something that's all your own. There are many ways to interpret each poem, and many ways to perform them. In any case, the foundation is set and the way is prepared for one to walk where they will.

A small but potent book of enlightenment, *City Prophet* exudes God's essence in identity and authority. Its pages turn with the breeze and its wisdom flies. It's a book that lives at home and breathes a life of its own. Zenith, its mouthpiece, stands in and atop the world, and speaks of what he sees. A view from having climbed the mountain and reached its summit; sight that mirrors the Maker all the way beyond. That spiritual essence and radiance is the province of the mystic's knowingness, and therefore transcends the conventions of religion. Herein, God is honoured and served both in name and in God's nameless reality – and is yours to embody if you deem it so.

TABLE OF CONTENTS

MISSION STATEMENT	i
A NOTE TO THE READER	iii
INTRODUCTION	1
THE BEGINNING	5
GOD	10
TRANSCENDENCE	14
INTUITION	16
PROMISED WORD	19
PASSION	21
PLEASURE AND PAIN	24
SEPARATION	27
MIRACLES	30
LOVERS	32
PARENTING	34
SILENCE	36
EMPTINESS	38
PATIENCE	41
SOCIAL AND SOLITARY	44
HONESTY	46
WISDOM	48

AWARENESS	50
AWAKENING	53
RICHNESS	56
CONTROL AND POWER	58
BEAUTY	61
THE DANCE	64
TEACHING	66
LOVE	69
LIGHT AND DARK	72
ENLIGHTENMENT	78
NOTHINGNESS AND ALLNESS	81
SALVATION AND ENLIGHTENMENT	87
THE CHRIST	91
THE END	96
AFTERWORD	100
AUTHOR'S BIO	105

INTRODUCTION

Our return to the power source sparks the greatest comeback. It's taken Man to go as far, for the Lord to come as close. God as I *and* You comes as was said. The servant's surrender to divinity itself, revealed in all fullness through the sovereign soul Self from poem 25-29. The life of Zenith reveals this over the course, in the same way as a flower that blooms in full when conditions ripen. Or, it could be said that for three days of the moons monthly cycle (one day either side of the full moon) its radiance shines to greatest effect. But it's the potency of those three days that culminates the entire cycle. Thus, the result in total, marks the absolute standing of truth of the Lord's manifestation into formation.

So, the divinity of power from poem 25 onwards, from its own vantage point, stands upon the shoulders of the parable preceding it. As that stance grew, so the shoulders strengthened with it. Before long, the body of work came into absolute proportion with how it stands. Overall, *the parable* transcends anything less than the ultimate reality of God.

The character of Reality, Zenith, is the spirit body: the vehicle and driver directing the masculine principle of the Godhead. Armi is the soul heart: the supporting role nurturing the feminine principle of God's heart. Christ is the creative spirit; the engine and producer, thus the role of Zenith as mystic and disciple is an unfolding creation of the eternal I – the model of the Maker.

CAVEAT

Witnessing the words of *City Prophet* changes lives. One's being and perspective may undergo a radical transformation. The alchemical process for the reader may at times feel more forced than willing, with time needed to assimilate the parable itself and the role in which the word of God plays through Zenith.

The revolutionary nature of the parable reshapes spiritual reality and religious devotion by clearing all the obstacles that obscure a direct experience with the Lord. Once Zenith achieves this, a bridge is built to help transport the saved soul to its enlightenment and beyond. The final step in this showdown of Transcendence (within the Kingdom of God – from poem 25-29) is taken by Christ himself, whose presence confronts the throng's perspective in such a way as to drive it to its peak, the greatest view.

THE BEGINNING

From the void, the dead of night, and across all stars bright, Zenith, God's mouthpiece, thus appears. His soul descends and lights a spark in the dark. A radiance that shines into human form. A blazed landing finds himself upon Melbourne, a city once most liveable and so loved now bleeds to death in bondage. Split and scarred from a thousand lashings forcing mass compliance.

A flicker of time passes. Zenith remembers the call. To the Yarra River his soul hovers, and the path beckons with craft made for all waters. It's rest day, predawn, and like a ball of light blazing the streets, he moves. Zenith's arrival meets joggers on the foot trail hugging the stream and birds chirping a symphony of songs. Lit bridges arch over the river, and tall lantern lights with oak trees aplenty side with it. The famed Alexandra Gardens provides the backdrop, and in the distance a mountainous city stretches across.

Poised upon the Morell bridge arching over the river, Zenith narrows his eyes on the misted setting. His craft sails close, somewhere off the docked bay. With no time to waste, he read the stars and charted the valleys. Time is near – his time! Gazing into endless night, he saw a little more: a vision of the souls of men, women, and children swirling the sky. Suddenly they approached his eye. They came dreaming for the life of wisdom earned. Many rode the wind: lucid and longing. Some flew on a wing and a prayer, while the rest just seemed altogether drawn.

Hundreds of souls hovering in the screen of his minds-eye. People like you and your neighbour huddled close. Zenith knew their ears were sharp, even if their eyes weren't. They wanted their piece of the puzzle and portion of pie. He obliged by giving them their share.

Raising high his head and spreading wide his arms, inspired breath filled him. To them he said, "You come in the night looking for light – for that one who stalks the sun. Then, if you will, lend your ear to this speech – my salute. In this vision, where your body rests and spirit soars, time has come to fear less and not at all, for this voice removes stench and freshens breath. I offer a fine taste and different flavour. All yours to chew on. Remember to eat, to get your fill. A strong stomach is needed to feel it all. And don't be shy to ask for more, for life gives endlessly.

"Life's longing, the heart of it, is yours to pass through. On the way, you'll meet death – the first and last of its kind. Your greatest eye salutes it goodbye. Homage paid to the hurt gone and healing come. Heed first your wants on fire and how fast they burn. Just add water for balance. This movement from wanting to longing is needed change. The pain moving there a blessing disguised.

"People of Melbourne, my love permeates our city as I hold you to my heart, blood wrenched. My eyes well watching you in light dimmed low. I see many torn from head to toe and ripped at the seams. Wounds weeping for a fallen city. Cut down by the crafty cat and dirty dog. Snakes slimming in and out of a public sermon, injecting poison into one's hallowed home. A paralysed panic and frozen fear. Inner talk growing like a beanstalk. Last rights up for grabs, hijacked by the house of horrors hosting. Freedom on the line. Walking the tightrope. I'm here to raise the bar and give it to you for balance.

THE BEGINNING

"I too, like you, have tarried the path of shackled feet and bound wrists. Now this soul swims afloat and dives beneath, free from drowning tyrants. Wind moves me as it does the ocean. Into wounded waters, I ride. My craft is coming and so too my love. We'll set sail for surgery. Cutting is my way. The result sows the river to its own.

Friends forsaken, but how can I leave you when we are as One? The sounding board behind this speech breathes my silken lips to speak by and for you. So, in memory, mine of Melbourne, I ask for you to take heed, making all feeling and thought salt that's pinched. What I've spoken needs no thinking to how it feels nor feeling to how you think. To say different finds logic out of place and feelings out of sorts. The result breeds a language lost in translation." Then, with a sigh of sadness, Zenith waved farewell.

Turning back, a fog haze paved way for his pathway incoming. The hum of the craft caressed his ear. His eyes welled a little more, for thereupon the craft in her solitude steering, stands Armi, his Other. Docked, Armi tied her ride and felt the rush: as did Zenith. Feelings deep coursed through and moved her to him, and him to her. A meeting of hearts as his speaks to hers.

"From hopeless to hopeful, from small belief to large faith, in mind, body, and spirit we meet. Because of you I came to be what I am. You are the greenhouse to all I plant. The one who walks with me through harsh terrain. One who swims my swim in a vicious sea. When I burn, you singe deep, and when you bleed, I run raw, like molten rock. We dream of hills and oceans alike, so seek I have for us a path stretching this river across. In commitment to my God, the same as yours, let's find rest then sail away."

A zephyr washed through. The trees shook with pleasure as spring seasons the air. And with the raw and real burning in each, his ear listened as her mouth spoke. "From the ocean deep to sand alone, upon a mountain crest to a sunken valley, in a city blaze or into the wild, my heart pours its music into yours. Time to rage silent for this party of One and move with the deepest dance. Let us ride and rock this river!" Hand in hand and heart in heart, both boarded the craft.

And on this day of rest, morning dawn lays bare a city moist with vaporous dew drops. Foregoing are the church bells! A ring sounding the forecast of a true coming. Its echo, striking and palpable shuddered through Melbourne's own. The dead came to life and the well-rested hopped to it. An awakening rose to the surface and spread. People from all walks and many faiths filled the city's centre. Clergymen and women from home and afar began assemblage of Melbourne's own.

In silent wait for the clergy to speak, up rose from the crowd a man. To them he said, "Today, we quench our thirst along a brook: one that runs high from a mountain and low to a valley. Today, this taste adds sugar and spice. These clothes I wear, torn like cloth, weaves its own thread and so must you. Aye, this affection that here so draws us, clergy leaders, prompt us with your speaking."

Then a priest came forth and said, "Fellow beings! Today we share a dream spawned from the same root. A sacred seed planted on enriched soil, and a stem bursting through with branches that reach. We've tasted the fruit and hunger for more. Let's soak into the river filling the banks in prayer. May our worlds meet the one with his craft."

In flocks, the clergy and people led the way. Through the city, they forged and along to the Gardens of Alexandra where the river's banks side. From the Morell Bridge, the arch of his speech, to high sense arena backing, the people assembled.

Light shone through as clouds paved way. The sky appeared imbued. In their droves, the gathering seated. Earth's grass the landing space and place. The whisper of worship swept across. Prayer began.

While within the prayer of their heart's content, a woman rose suddenly, mumbling loud to the heavens and the Earth and to all in her firing line. Incoherent and dishevelled, she was rebuked by many. Just as suddenly she sat, calm as a millpond. It was at that very moment that a child stood tall and silent, pointing towards the river at its bend. Others caught the child's meaning, wondering what laid beyond. A few boys and girls ran to the mount where the river curved. The great unknown all too appealing not to know.

"There he is! Here he comes!" shouted one of the girls. She waved high out to the craft, and in her greatest voice she called out saying, "Devoted one, I saw you and this in a dream. We stand with you. Can you speak to us some more, if only a little?"

Zenith motioned Armi to come close and closer still. Undaunted and bold, he joined her atop where all steers. Awe gripped him at once as he marvelled at the sight of souls hungry for food and thirsty for drink. Deeply moved, the air Zenith gave breath to churned a force reckoned within. With passion charging through, he spoke – a large voice.

"Today in your wake, I, Zenith, answer the call of you, my brothers and sisters of Melbourne. Through you, what I say already stirs. Every sound ringing true, pulsates from a hollow body, and speaks to silence over clapping hands. Today, the strings of your heart pull untied, and now the rush of blood blows its gift through me. A present I pay forward with eyes to show for it and a voice to cut through. Truth will cast a mirror. Contrast will show when the seer sees it all as is."

Before all, on the waters above, his craft hovered and the ripples waved. The setting deepened. Colour vivid and rich flourished throughout. The skies touch descended as the craft came to rest. Surveying the grassland, Zenith caught vision of talk engaged between the clergy. Moments later a priest, acting as a speaker for the people, said to Zenith, "Speak to us of God."

1. So he responded swiftly to say, "Deny the devil and death its day, affirms God as you in every way. When your imperfect is perfect, you are flawed no more, like God no less: leaving well enough alone for the great unknown. It gives space and grants time for time for your walk with the wounded. Strength to embrace your own this very moment. A far cry from those too hard to reach.

2. "Why deny so long what our hand is made to hold? Clutching at straws when time calls for a strong arm. May the wonders of shame drown the shameless to teach the lesson of giving God all your time.

3. "Even if God split a strand of hair in two, both take root when we see each as One. No such thing as split ends on Godhead's end. Shaved or not, I present a face shaped by none of it. This world and I facing off, for what cuts with prunes better when worlds no longer preside.

4. "When God paints His shape, it becomes art set for life. And when life walks off the canvas, and one step

of that foot grounds upon the path you lay, your stride also would come to life, balanced and restored. A nimble foot and light imprint since this world is no stomping ground.

5. "God is the First and Last. All in truth recedes or proceeds to God. One way or the other we begin where we end. And our best takes the time to open and close what we must start and finish. Death to my*self* for a life of God's wealth. See beyond what's seen. Be beyond what's been. I'm saying now before the moment's gone. To go there, to dig up the present, we cut with the past to sew up the future. Forever times it as all the same. Nature is that basic, and grace nurtures its growth watching it grow: even watching grass grow.

6. "Some seek God in edifice moulded of rock and brick. Then let that be your home. Live there than so visit. I go to this place throughout the day. God is my church. When worshipped, no gap wedges this from that. It's either This or it's That.

7. "Time to crash the house built to fall. Removed for a better version using home hardware. Wreckage all around, unfound on fertile ground. And when building, structure aligns if fitted right. Even in death this process deems itself creative. Right to say too that Creation is served in God's own Self through ours. But to destruct through a lens less vast acts out the difference of it. If you must, for the sake of order anew, let loose chaos, moving up and down *with* what

is. The same choice dismantles all that claims to be what never can.

8. "Truth like this just crops up. Heaven placed the seed underground, in the Earth as much as over the stars, in her womb as much as in his brain. Pay homage for your footing while riding the rainbow, for she harvests whatever weather he colours. A stallion and mare gallop. Their offspring forms life well beyond gender.

9. "For now O strangers upon strange land and friends on home soil, kickstart by quenching your thirst. A drink into the night drunk on the stars. Blast into inner space. A rocket through to the Earth within. Her womb is as heavenly as her land. To be as close belongs you with her and her with you, knowing the land of hers and of ours stretches of its own. To this, God would say, "I am Earth and she is Mine." So, if the stars call out from where you stand, then see Heaven all the same. Above *as* below.

10. "Unleash your primal roar, the heart of fire. Courage, my friends, the burning deep awaits. The unstoppable fall flashing past. The moment came down with it, hitting right between the eyes. On target for sight sharpened right. Fire charging life and fire burning it. Creation seeded and destruction when needed. The passion emancipates. Freedom of this kind propels. From star to star, spring-loaded and leaping, the webbed matrix nets but thin air. You unbound therein jumps inside the grid-work and frames it right. If not, if star and light are torn in two, how can the

ying of all stellar and stuff feel it true? Watch out for the yang splitting credit. This yang owes – a self in debt. Be rather with the yang giving all and the ying receiving no less. There's always profit to this.

11. "The rising of God much emanates from the moon's hidden side. Black holes shining depth. A source drawing blood from its own in a heart beating for it. The face of this ying and yang forms two sides of the one coin. Flip it anyway you like, the moon shines. All dreams true in this wishing well. No coins gold plated.

12. "Come with me to the wellspring and youth fountain, outpoured from whence it came. May life rise in such a way. Like the tree whose sap bears fruit. When we drink its flow and eat its substance, mouth-watering clarity moves. Its essence is to be savoured. And for this we bin illusion. Tastes like rubbish!

13. "Eating to our fancy and swallowing for real – consumed by Mother Earth's token meal. She pleases human need, feeding even the sickest weed. Medicine planted from rain and dirt. What comes prior to the seed shooting forth goes without word. Never can that word know which is. What can be said is we took root for growth bearing all to come to their own: to come grounded and fertile through the love and know-how of Heaven upon Earth."

TRANSCENDENCE

From the crowd, a witness rose. His gaze pierced into Zenith's own. Others caught the meaning of this stilled sharing. The man then looked to the crowd and with intent he said, "To he I turn to scratch the itch, to knead our sore spot. The wound runs deep. Power needed to suck the pus and surge from a bottomless pit. Will he rise to drop our issue? Will he reach beyond and speak of its Transcendence?"

1. And before more, Zenith spoke, "In the limits of mind your problem grows, and beyond it the solution sows. To wake up to it, put mind to rest. To rest into it, wake up to mind. Sharpened sight is your tool to carve a thought and cut it too. Off with the head with a smooth slice of the skin, or serrated, if you must. Then the answer under the axed mind will shine, cutting through at once. No messing with the question or answer – who needs problems!

2. "Leave the search to be itself. Just watch. No word, no sound, no self! Need I say more, but I will: silence *is* the answer never come nor gone. What pervades *is* always *in* all ways. Free of here and anywhere not-here. What left is there to be above and within of?

Transcendence then, its very expression means God's immanence is accounted for.

3. "To draw inspired breath and rise above, look around. Touch the nearest tree. Feel her trunk on you. She leans in, giving to and drawing from the root of her seed. Similarly, you give best drawing blood from the marrow, bleeding and breathing from within and without.

4. "Creation beyond evolves within. Above the world and all the way in it leaves life unchanged in a changing world. That said, the seed needs planting to find the flower. Its being becomes it when the flower comes to bloom. And when that time comes, that is when nature speaks and you listen, all told remains the least bit. The know-it-all looks within the word. Who *does* know parts clouds at one end and lies beneath the other. The ups and downs of above and below meeting in the middle from nowhere special: from nowhere at all.

5. "Even so, the greatest of that leap gathers dirt. Still, that leap now-here and from it, even to worlds away, spring cleans and makes a chemical stir in the process. Substance alone sucking poison to death. In whatever demise, benign or tragic, the cure comes eyeing the speck of Earth gone blue."

INTUITION

Zenith surveyed the setting. Vision thrived before him. A scene of people emerged of which one said, "Such madness made of such sense. This man's mind is lost and another found. If I'm not making sense, you're crazed. O voice of reason, speak also on Intuition."

1. He said, "Intuition goes north, instinct south. A human in spirit and an animal in soul. A sound mind follows, along with all reason. I'll start above, spiritual, and end below, primal: Must we tear at the skin to feel inside? Must we rip open the stomach to get gut instinct? What good's a body without mind, let alone soul? Beware the brains' trust, who thinks they know. Since I'm here in Soul and Spirit, how are we to come to what the brain alone cannot? First, wise up and get your act together, letting good faith abide. Even those denied of faith have it for denial itself. Negation belying sense, if truth be told. Lacking touch, and out of touch. Sensation far from the crux of sense.

2. "And would these words alone be as discerned if *this* vehicle created life? I'm not that small. So, make these words but yours to peel or shred. Throw away

like dead bark. That image is nobody's fool. Past the picture gets it: gets body-*wise*. How else to flesh it out and break it down? For starters, here is my body of work... Eyes piercing into I. Ears closed empty's noise. Skin roused feeling inside. Scent caught by the nose that knows. Touching that turns soul inside out... Knowing this reveals faith, and faith in it reveals it known.

3. "High time I became madness divine in every sense of the word. Mistakes aplenty to stake their claim on this word and that. Whose fault is that? Who lost their head or fault-found it? Both are caught in a senseless act. It's hard for the mind to get its head around – imperfect means I'm-perfect. Mindset provides the tools, and brains the skill to read it in-sight.

4. "Whatever *your* device, use it to pierce through. Hurt it may. A little discord or a lot may beat your pulse. There's the moment to pound hard and the moment to soften it. Feel it all and all the way through. It's just a feeling. Ride that wave with patience. Nightfall brings in the tide and strips it down. All to bathe a body and wash the mind. With the day done and dusted and all senses settled, there's just a candle left and a song to flame it. Listen close and you'll hear a formless note tuning form with feelers for arms and the smarts on brains to intuit it.

5. "Now to beauty in the beast. Feelings aside and all thoughts too, the animal sniffs out the human you. If it's right or wrong or yes or no, below the navel tells

it so. In the body and out the mind is yours and my deepest find. The temple stands tall and wise, for the truth never lies.

6. "Monsters all and evil too, when the basement's locked and the cave's taboo. Lamb without lion is like a dandelion. So harmless it's dangerous, its weed grows cancerous. Intuition feels the flower, and instinct smells its power. The former merges, the latter purges. In the cycle of life and death, there's a spiritual sense lacking breath. Inhaling deep and low realigns with the flow. Primal passion and power too that owns the beast within you. This belly beneath has my trust over everything above my thrust. The animal innate is my soulmate. God disguised in a panther's eyes."

PROMISED WORD

Zenith continued saying, "This speech is of its own. I dare not give my word to it, as its way leaves its own mark and signs off accordingly. Shall I go on?" Many rose in favour. "Then what will you have me speak?" One stood tall saying, "Be it the Promised Word."

1. He said, "Silence is greater than any word. Every word we present comes to pass. So too our value stocked in a promised morrow. If you must say so, "I'll do it" says enough. Anything more than silence after is overpriced and less than promising. Drop the vow and act now. Your essence shows how, how a promised land stands. Short of that sparks a takeover on foreign soil. God's home sold to the highest bidder promising more than delivered. Short of that, one's heart and drive, talks big and acts small.

2. "Little substance and principles too. Is this you? Is this your worth? If not, if the land you own is valued to rise, still I ask: on what grounds is your worth framed?" A city dweller said, "On wasted lands, if truth be told." A policeman said, "In power and force, law bound." And a judge said, "In justice upheld and hammered down." Zenith said, "Living that, your

truth today brings life your way. Whose walk talks, no one knows more than its way. The next move unknown until in it. All else rides the morrow hard today, pledging this oath and that act on shifting grounds.

3. "This is spoken to puncture pride and build courage. Each word truth speaks instructs on how it's known. There's no catching the essence of it. Anything caught or freed are easily grasped. Truth is something else no word can know. No words over-promised or under-supplied. Just the power to rise over this word or that vow and put the land of the free to use. But before that day comes, brittle remains must turn to dust and rise again stronger and tough. Bare bones ready for crunch time in the promise of trust."

PASSION

Lit ablaze by a spark, soul filled the air. The mood moved; so much so for one to ask, "What takes us this deep and so high?"
   "The fire" one yelled.
   "Yes, our passion." another said.
   Then a voice called out saying, "I urge for you, Zenith, to speak on Passion."

1. He said, "Passion's aim strikes while it's hot. Easy to throw caution to the wind when emotion's involved. Watch the arrow tipped in fire and beware your motive sent forth. Needless attack sets fire to all, leaving nothing but a burnt wound.

2. "I'm not here to dampen proceedings or to inflame them. Any fool can wage war, but open fire takes years of skill. Is any battle worth playing with fire? If you must take aim, hit the target. Missing the mark draws anger or reveals it. So, when anger or rage is what it is, feel the heat and move on, lessoning worry. And bless the good, and not as good. Not every arrow strikes dead on, but a wound well received bleeds and clots right.

3. "Passion takes well to air needing it. Balanced with water, desire moves where it should. You tell me,

what appeals more: a dormant volcano or one alive with molten lava? Careful, eruption implodes as much as explodes. When liquid lights viewed right, anger and aggression can move mountains. But be sound about it – pre-rational and post-intellect. Mindful of instinct and wise to all reason.

4. "Now to the guts of it: nature goes wild, and wolves must eat. This beast hunts for more brain. Full-bodied brute strength; a dragon breathing fire. How this creature smacks, sounds all too human. At this point, names matter not. Just the question of who is riding who – the dragon you, or you the dragon? One burns with light and the other is set alight. Know the difference and the danger, or go up in flames.

5. "If it sounds harsh then grate on it. Challenge back what does to you. Get those hands dirty. Grease and grime for the love of it. A sacred plough shovels shit, absorbs the smell, and sniffs it out. It's a stinking process: going where the sun don't shine. Heavy going outweighs a light load. Payment for a decent job slogging through, straight ahead as much as narrow. Each footprint leaving its mark patterned before us, our very eye.

6. "Eager to soar, it's time for air. The flight begins in earnest. Purpose supplies the fuel and intent the power. A rocket to the moon and back; all in a day's work. Others who fly into trouble, caught in a flat spin, ejection is small relief for a head in the clouds.

7. "Something must die to really live. Wreckage burnt to dust only to hit the ground running. Your sacrifice drives it and pays later down the road. Many checkpoints assessing the path. Roadblocks aplenty barricade the way. The bottom line cut off until cometh the man, cut-throat. Skilled talent executes it. Death by desire carried out in full.

8. "As *you* sojourn through this and that, may the fruits of your talent ripen. And when so would you rise to give those seeds in service? Or do your deeds need sit in glory's seat? Watch out, the rug pulls hard from beneath. Life exposes lives at just the right time. All to end yours out of line. Must dig in and carve the course, straighten up and steer the horse.

9. "Taking reign drives impulse and rides on a wave. Courage to surf the crest to the shore. Secrets from the deep tell how. In the dark down there, evils nowhere. No way to know unless you go. You want passion, a power most intense? Take in you, the ocean, and hold it there. Strength to lift heavy, and weight to carry light. "O keepers of the burning heart, with desire come and gone and the path restored, treasure lights up the ocean floor. Gold that struck in a blaze of glory and launched soul on fire across the world."

PLEASURE AND PAIN

Many shed tears of glee. A delight in light over dark. Some too dimmed from up high to low depths, cut down from sky and grounded on land. Then a young man said, "I beckon you, Zenith, please speak a word or two on Pleasure and Pain."

1. And he versed, "Pleasure has wings that span in flight, seeking within for endless night. Gates of heaven so very nigh, pleasure is freedom with a bottom tie. Some strive to be bold and free, chasing highs and feelings glee. Heed, hearts feel the weight and strain, upon pleasures young, fearful pain.

2. "Our pain is not for disdain, and pride in it strutting its stance is bound to fall. Who are we to lord above what sits beneath? Watch out for judgment come in humble guise. Nothing but a mask in hiding. I'm here to blow its cover. Idiots numb over feeling it. Scared stiff from all that bubbles skin deep. Hurt stuffed in a swell of all sorts. Where else can pain travel but buried?

3. "Pain suppressed, what a drain! Pain expressed, *watch* it, this human beast. Its grief lifts when you do. It takes a handle on hurt to rise to the challenge. Peace

with pain for even you most upset. Otherwise just a pain or a fool inviting it. Seeking pleasure to excess suffers it. Joy no more than it seems. A stirring rouse waxing pain for pleasure. Peace wanes and protests the process. Any claims of inciting are unmet. How let alone why when such stirring stills it too?

4. "There's a house in which we dwell, a temple in fact, that's well-furnished on solid grounds. A setting where we ride the wind on land and soil. Leaves they come and go and branches break. Each cycle takes root. The seasons speak of nature filled – of Earth breathing to live.

5. "Open and aired for soul to inspect, for soul to walk the land and swim the ocean, laying eyes on all seen. And what temple houses no stairway: steps mapping the terrain of both heaven and hell? Up the stairs, meet with the door saved just for you. Wide open to those opened wide. In the highlands we stand tall, bowed by eyes that kneel. Landscape as lavish as we let. Yet we must prove our trust. Faith in arms spread for a view as vast. No time like now to welcome whatever you feel, and all felt will greet you the same. What room is left for pain to dwell when your tears blow with the wind?

6. "Pain is the root of desires unmet. A plant meets itself when planted. When seeds stem desire moves. A greenhouse displays vision. What starts with you becomes a movement. Else desire alone shivers – a body wracked with pain. Tarry no longer upon pastured

grief. Time to take stock then reap the harvest. Thrust your best when ripe for pleasure. And, for this, focus turns in and sets the course. Drive it home! That way pain flounders to joys flourish.

7. "Companions of Communion, long have people en masse cried, 'When will pain have its end?' And I say to turn over if you will a heart pained. But to cry no more must it please the Absolute for which you seek. Thus, the heart which warms its pain grieves on compassion's ground. Each teardrop waters the way. Earthed by that which knows how to bear and to share. This seeping soul is sap bursting and fruit yielding. Carry on, even if all branched withers and dies. Burst at the seams yourself. Yielding yields less than zero.

8. "There's an ear given to sap talking as she gathers from her roots. It is too a pleasure for the seed spawned to bestow its gift to sap, as sap conveys with love. Sap is the bearer, joyous at receiving from the trunk as much as she is by giving to its leaves. So, may the pleasure and pain of your needs be as owned and as grounded. Lest shooting skyward be cut down to size."

SEPARATION

Cut to the bone, heads dipped and faces hid. His words all too much for some to take. Zenith caught the eye of them wounded and torn. Moved by what he saw, his head bowed for a moment as if to look within.

1. "He then said, "We separate just by means of flesh. To you split down the middle or any which way, feel the gap through light *and* dark. Much space or a little, allures the union state. What tears at the seam invite's sewing. Wounds heal in their own time and so will you. Pain needs to rise to the surface. Feel its pinch and its gash. Its way gets under the skin and out of it. But we must shred a whole cut to allow so. Lest we hurt others as much ourselves.

2. "The call comes to leave the foe for the friend. Those who deserve get just that. O shadowed one, give thanks for the truth laid bare and I'll pay back your due respect. Let's pull in the same way and run with it. That's what oils the engine and ignites the spark. The charge is electric. We're meant to exhaust and fuel again. Intensity has its price. Who buys it pays it. Here's all I have, my last coin. Here's all I bleed, my last drop.

3. "A motor this powered demands a driver focussed straight and ahead. No cutting corners or wavering eyes. No right verses wrong way." Suddenly a doctor spoke saying, "But what future for those sliced up and smashed hard? How may they heal from such pain?" Zenith answered, "Tension unties by kneading the knots and eyeing the feeling. Fools look away, too wrapped up in the moment and the morrow. Gripping too tight tears it apart and leaves a soul unravelling. Letting go loosens the load. How it's done matters not. With bloody hands, if you must. What's wrong? Does the sight of blood turn your head? Denied pain suffers it. Get surgical and operate. Open heart surgery is fancied. Healing the sick cuts an open wound. Look within to where it beats. Nothing needs stitching when breathing airs. Life, the lungs only need."

4. And a train driver said, "Like the doctor, I came today dressed to serve. But how to drive uniform when the course severs?" Zenith answered, "Station and express go together. Since when has the carriage of non-doing ever detached from what does? The wheel always turns when even still. It's a narrow path, this life. Easy to slip off the rails. Know when to apply the brakes. And beware also the scenic route and winding track. Distraction makes steering hard. Such veering brings smoke and soot. Eyes suffer the haze. Blinded from the truth of the matter, sadness wells up. Best to pass that memory on and go the direct route. It's bliss we miss. All pieced together equals peace.

5. "To be that clear, keep watch. All that rises and sets comes to pass. Still the sun shines and so must you. Else watch your skill decline too. Like a chainsaw carving ham, fools use the wrong tool for the job. No use blaming your tools. What's going on upstairs? A few loose screws? Shake it empty. Get to the rust before it rots. A new set of tools will do. Must I hammer this? Okay, get to work crafting life. Here's a tip to nail it: melt hand into hammer into hand.

6. "It's fluid, this life. Flowing with the go and the slow adapts to the groove and the unmoved. Likewise, real change hits those unchanged by it. Stilled, even in the face of fear, staring down the void and strengthened to keep going, straight ahead, all the way, no matter what. We've all made noise when scared. Lightning storms and thunder claps when thinking over feelings. If you're sad, be sad! Anything less is absent – neither real nor unreal. So be true. Peace upon you who are, even you most upset.

7. "Reality bites and fiction swallows. Both seem to eat at separate tables. Another look catches both dining hand in hand. No backs turned when you've got each other's. What's reality without fiction to colour it? Likewise, I tell a story for truth's own glory. But for you who want it plain, prose alone poses a problem. Boredom from it split through, piece by piece. Cut from the reed to longing starved of soul. Hungry for the whole slice and every piece of the entire cut."

MIRACLES

Moments later, children came to light. Attention fixed upon them. Blazing auras could be seen by many close and afar. Each child gazed the grid. Then one, a mouthpiece for their voice said, "Teacher, we came today hungry, hoping to be fed. Your food feeds in ways that ask for more. This time a word, if you will, on Miracles."

1. He spoke, "Let Earth be your chef. Watch how she makes no meal of it. Whatever the season, she gets it done. Nature served on a platter. How on Earth could there be a better host? Such delicate taste. The secret ingredient – okay, I'll tell it straight: the recipe is blessed with real magic.

2. "*A* miracle is a budded flower blossomed. *The* miracle is a budded flower moved to blossom. Whoever wants alchemy shovels dirt for it. That we're digging into the dark is courageous enough, but to upturn trampled turf is another matter. But then, gold patrons deal with life in-depth. Skim over at your peril. How marvellous to find dirt as treasured gold.

3. "Best to be quiet than spread pearls to filth. Let walking do the talking. Moving with purpose. No

room left for eyes to wander. No room left off-course at all. Signs and wonders cross the path straight and small. Winding all over the place breeds a drunken mess. At that point, praying for a miracle won't help. Straighten up and buckle down – there's your miracle! Just rise with all that's had. Compassion gets it done and comedy makes it fun. Morning glory when limber inside out. Or flip the script to what was and watch a horror show unfold. Green splatting tomatoes coming your way.

4. "I could sprout a course in miracles or just move from morning dew to the still of day longing, content with it and the life planned. Or further still, let's move to dusk shaking off the day's dust, and refresh the same in twilight hours. For night, just like day, heralds a dream for something new and something true. Just take rest within."

LOVERS

Two women rose, hand in hand they said in unison, "Speak of us – Lovers."

1. And he said, "When I speak of lovers, its namesake starts with love, then so must I. Love so the lover as love is so, giving more and your all. Be wary too of the expectant you. It comes laden with pain when wanting much gain. Love breaks the mould for soul to shape. How *we* formed is a mystery. I'm unknown to myself, let alone you. But to keep mystique then dive as deep as the descent demands and come for air next season.

2. "By sharing life, freedom and love must be open to each. For what is free without love breeds license, and what is love without freedom enslaves. Remember to rise above when falling in love. Going down's not much fun unless you're up to it. And when two hearts meet in deep embrace, both beat in each and in pace. But theirs isn't yours to own. Possession stifles. Who wants bondage, less leather and lace, or a shouting match filled with time-outs?

3. "You, hand in hand and those strolling just the same: let summer shine the space between your footsteps and hers. When autumn falls and trees weep, may the sap in you bleed too. All we shed comes to pass, like the leaf on the grass. When winter rains, may you both rest, warming love. Nurture each to comfort. Perhaps a blanket for the weary worked. Not too many layers, for every heart needs room to breathe. With spring in the air, gardens glow as colour pops. Nature, she draws us out and calls us in. A solitary walk, so the heart can pound strong, choosing flowers for the one so longed. Like two souls who would connect than so touch; let the four seasons encompass you both. Lovers relate well when walking on sand with spacious footsteps."

PARENTING

Two men rose, with one saying, "May you spread more your speech, this time on Parenting."

1. He said, "Huff and puff away, your child lives their stay for the day no other way. All that steam wiped clean when family gleams. Our sons and daughters demand us here and now. But give, too, yourself the moment as you would your child. Raise the ways of parentage as *you* would. Benefit pays your way. And when growth sprouts in them and you, that's life making itself anew. Eyes on you and yours on them, looking to you for some clue.

2. "As you teach, so do they themselves learn. Parents fumbling through and children kicking and screaming. Or parents honouring the master and children the disciple. Whether it's hard and tough or smooth and easy, or all else in between, together you are kindred beyond the family name. Each member uniquely you and the same like you.

3. "Strive to where our children thrive. Even you parent-free may carry the instinct. A parental figure to that one who tugs your heart, cocooned in a seed

of promise. As your paths meet, get serious too and discipline before it gets too serious. And if it does, may the joker at play find a way, bringing parent to child the one within. You'll age well, as will your offspring, letting loose the reigns. Just enough for freedom to season. Its sacred space needed for kinship to strengthen and ripen to fruition."

SILENCE

Huddled close, a group of monks gestured to each other. Suddenly one rose, a champion for those knelt. With bowl in hand she outreached saying, "Feed us more this Silence, and the way to it."

1. Zenith said, "The way to silence is but a way. Short and thin, this speech. Odour wafts when words linger. Fungi spews all over the much ado talker. Yes, bullshit babbles beating around the bush. You can't fool me with speech, dropping words in bucketloads. Try it! I'll throw it back, the mirrors view. My end looks clear doesn't it, if you stopped to notice. Either way you won't see me for dust.

2. "Quiet the chatter and patter within. Words irritate, scrubbed any old way. Skills brushed up hold things in good stead. Rubs the right way crafting speech. The work begins behind the scenes backing the sounding board and platform. An ear to the ground clears the decks in one fell swoop. It came from nowhere. Life gives and it takes. Nothing handed on a platter. Empty plates are where it starts. Food lives there. This deal isn't just a meal. Flavour to it gives style and spice.

Cook or go hungry; whichever captures the essence you savour.

3. "Exquisite sense delights in food and the plate it's on. No time for talk, eating says it all. Such pleasure dining with peace and quiet. And so I say to move far thy focus from tasted speech. If we must speak, let it be said but that it lasts.

4. "Spirit speaks if listened, and nudges if felt. From no point or place, sensing aims it true. A direct hit knows the way forward and where it's been. Actions doing the talking. Speaking it crosses the mind ill focussed. I'm making no point but to say something so you don't. It's your time-out from this thought and that. No more thoughts galore or an insane brain. Better to cut off your ear and tongue than lose your head. Part ways with one thought and a thousand more. You'll know all you know letting go.

5. "There's a time to give to the search and a time to give it up. I must shoot forth, shutting up shop, and leave this world and that for something more. A strap in for the trek over the moon and stars. Doing so won't get done just doing. We've got to *Be* to get I, me, and the Lord O Thee. I could go on, but best to spread space, a gap and slide down beneath all word and sound."

EMPTINESS

A man then said, "This silence fills and it empties. The Emptiness, must he speak of it?"

"Yes," hailed the crowd.

1. Zenith said, "Each desert has its land, and each space its place. So, what is empty has its fill. Diverse in times adverse ups the value as prices plummet. Tough times makes those tough. Strength in clocking hours. It cuts time – voids it. The void made valid. Not a void dead to life, but one made for life.

2. "Where no-thing resides homes everything that counts. There's a chief in charge of those quarters. Soldiers all, at attention and at ease. No stopping from where it's marched. Zero excuse for going nowhere. Inspection resolves the search. Barren land up for grabs. Emptied of this and that for something more. And founded from that place erased. Why rush it, the reaching, when within grasp – in even one's palmed hand?

3. "Time siding with those born of patience. Cuts baggage down to size. Not a moment more lugging

such a load. Adding to what's empty wastes time, not to mention space. And time is not for waste. Build a legacy fit with many doors. Each opened to a mystery more than before. Make people work for *real* estate. And for that a key is needed. Cut it to *your* size. Now there's a perfect slot no matter what. But it takes the right turn to move with the hollow groove. It's got to click. You who hit it off, come take a peek and watch the drama unfold. Life and death face to face in deep embrace.

4. "We all have in us a fire raging close, for the intimate, where the world blows away like flour in the wind. Down deep in the heart of it, no frills or fluff working with essence. Why sprout an embellished account? It spreads weeds and misleads. Must dig and put in the groundwork before an issue fastens root. Cleared of weeds room abounds, ready for growth. No time to reflect on rotten remains. Why raise a stink that lingers? The smell leaves a pained face. Who needs the hurt, haunting those deadened by it? Pain sought sours it more. Leave the dead be where they are. Graves are no place to live.

5. "We come to life filled of it. Some call the glass half full, others the glass half empty. I say nothing by half measures amounts to much. Being full is as empty as it gets, and being empty gets it as full. Two sides, one moon, formed and void of it all the same. The moon emptied from sight. It wasn't a magic trick. Life expressed flipped back within to unexpressed.

6. "Well-watered, gardens grow absent of nothing no more. All plantation feeds on work. No absence of leave required. No downtime needed. The root of it is paid its due and returns the favour. The cheque voids only that of no worth. That way pockets are emptied and business thrives."

PATIENCE

Up and geared, an electrician said, "Charged by a burning core, air surges forth. The power grid sparks. And for all who feel the juice electrifies the current. What's wired goes without name. Still its source bears with all names rung true. Now its name, one of foremost, I send to you giving. 'Tis for me to pass on the fill coursing through. Just as the dream foretold: be for who it must and so it is. Zenith, bless us with what you say on Patience."

1. He said, "Patient, O patient: you are soap made to scrub. Rags old and torn are used and tossed to waste. Restored cloth favoured too for that clean wipe. A kind hand that takes the time. No sum of dirt and grime sees you whine.

2. "Who grounds as good? For that, Earth is most tended. Fire seasoned is, too, your friend soaring a slow burn. Water streamed and seeped pours and endures in much your way. Some, hurried, pull hair and pluck feathers, but you breathe long and deep. Every need entrusted and supplied. Appeased by the resolve to reach all the way, whichever way.

3. "Tenacity's your tool, serenity's your song, and the way in which you move... Grace, your lover and

mate, footing an elegant dance. Yes, you belong to this very day, composed and composer. How else can poetry's pen dazzle bereft of your hand? The greatest of readers read, and writers wrote. All rights to the book inked with deep wonder and awe. Life published in real print. Nothing cooked up. Just the strength to eat from soul fully raw."

4. Suddenly, one restless and young cried out, "Heard I have of us a bond born hidden. Why befriend me your foe who hasn't time to rhyme? Slowing down lags along. How these fetters drag! My rage in spite is purpose filled. Like the hair that bolted I get things done. Still, I fall flat. Why am I pressed down and judged poor?"

5. "Quiet," said Zenith firmly. "You see this young fool? These bring best the wise to counsel. Your need for speed flies further than patience allows. Life on full throttle can heed the red flags. But your impatience drives right by them. The difference is small at high speeds. The margins tight when judgment loosens. Heed the signs to gear down, or crash the next moment. Stopped in your tracks without warning. Life hits and worlds weigh. See the mirror of yours.

6. "I *appear* you your foe. Those sly would have me circle in your mix. But if you, mixed up, come true for help, then who am I to strain or drain you? For the moment, shake out of it and break free the shackles of conscience. Paradox and dualism are caged turf. Dig deeper. Unearth all graves sporting death. Laid bare

beneath, the secret opens. The truth's out without a moment's notice. Nature has its time. Be on watch for the harvest. Seasons may pass before results reap. But for the one diligent and steady, the time will come, even as we speak.

7. "By virtue of patience has virtue ascendant and atop. Virtue this high is more than common. Watch closely these and how each extends. Real reaching knows what to do and doesn't ado with don'ts. Therefore, do with non-doing, for such virtue gets it done. Quick, idle ways waste your time, not to mention mine. Waste smells. Then, just as suddenly, time is yours when stench turns to scent."

SOCIAL AND SOLITARY

Urgent and pleading, a beggar said, "Devoted one, help weigh even the scales. Relieve this burden between us our Social self and us in Solitude."

1. Zenith said, "When the sun shines on you, you alone feel it and it alone feels you. Its light is given to warm you, I and the world over. How happy are you, soothed even more in the light of all suns? Such radiance gives back and pours out, touching all near as much as dear. Presence made to sizzle and burn. Who can't handle the heat burns out. Who can't keep up wastes your time. Go it alone or at least your own way. Happy alone by day and by night and happily not, just the same.

2. "Whatever the case, the day is yours and yours alone to exhaust and fuel. Challenge the day as it does to you. Heavy hitting is how it works. No tougher companion than life. When dusk nears, life softens and gives a setting sun to replenish with. When night falls, silence calls. It sounds like an ocean inside. Walk the tide and feel the trickle, the rush of water and the sand. Where the moon shines, move with it. Chase the shadows away! When the moon sits, rest with it for some peace and quiet.

3. "Even these seashells, an ocean they swam to be by and with you. Are their calls to befriend harkened to? The ocean whistles through them their story to the ear given. Beached empty and alone recalls home well and good. To be that social and as sourced, feed lone time and its longing.

4. "Some still ask of why such need to be alone than with others? I say it's a tug, yes, a tug calling me and my need for solo flight, to move away far to be so close, giving, giving. Give to you yourself time and space. You would others, then yourself.

5. "Whispers speak loud, holding ground, but it takes silence to hear such music and sound. Song and dance poured forth through strings of a humming heart. If no longer can you keep in your heart, drive then to stirring tongues and kissing lips. Such lips vibrate tone alone and shares with how it tastes. One sound in a mouthful. Listen within or go without. Hearts beating *with* the head of the process. Alone to what if sound and silence score at once?"

HONESTY

From shaded ground, despair cried, "Long has speech lashed my tongue. A slave whipped by others and self. All I chew spews glass. A mouthful of cuts and splinters tell the truth. They say there's no fix without my help."

"Woe betide you," scoffed another. "A hopeless cry drowned in tears. Hurting with little outreach. Desperate, but not for help. If you did come in two minds, one for help and one sabotaged, may you leave different in one mind just. I too, like you, lost my head and near my soul but for the one rung true. Through a brave descent, shadows lifted. It took a long look and hard edge. An honest account that cut to the core. Zenith, blessed in truth are we if you would speak on Honesty."

1. Zenith replied, "It's a jungle in here – tree bound and deep rooted. Not for any to just swing on by. To cut to the truth, handle the elements. Else run headlong into branch upon branch and lie upon lie. Killing nature because of yours. Hold breast-plated your hand. Honestly, how devoted are you? Integral growth needs a heart for the job. It's the right thing to bring and it's also the kindest. Attend to it as nature intends. If the heart considers your truth worthy, still, have you with that settled lax with your lot? Best to laze

least from our laurels or suffer the sloth. The cost is an honest living on the line.

2. "If truth be known, getting honest carves it up and deals it raw. It means cutting through. But not to the quick: that hurts! Within, speaks a truth that's yet heard. Tend to it and you in turn will be as tended. Give your all to it and all returns as given. All gets its fill when fulfilled. No*body* goes starved feeding guts an honest serving.

3. "Any way you slice it, the eyes tell if you're lying. Look for deceit devouring the dish, or a story cooked up. That's no way to cook. Food poison ensures – sickened from the bite cutting deep. A bandage won't do to cover the mess. See inside the wound cut open, acquainting oneself with bare bones and raw nerves. If *you* won't, your hurt will. This the moment of truth: bad blood cuts until sowed, and scabs until healed. Venom to swallow and stomach. Such honesty, not everyone's serum."

WISDOM

An aged man said, "This stick with which I walk, as I ground it so is it my grounding. O you may think I am struck down, brittle, shaking in my boots. If only you knew my cane is my wand. I make no show of it. Seize it from whence it came and those shall be seized. Its power knocks senseless force that steals. It comes upheld with what makes sense and strikes down in a flash. The hard and fast of lessons learnt teaching wisdom.

"Zenith, speak to us of it – Wisdom."

1. He said, "The air of wisdom and wisdom aired freshens mystique. Its scent arrives when the world departs. Presence in the world's absence. Neither this wise nor that, the wise spring forth prior to this and that. From *I am that*, to *I am*, to *I*.

2. "Wisdom grows from all things Known. That it grows is enough. And when so, that is, when life hits and yours takes the punch, your story stands, even one so sad. For sadness turns suddenly glad of the experience gained.

3. "Where others stunt growth and snap like twigs, you who plants anew and matures the crop reaps the harvest. Progress showing your know-how. Presence

given than that of words. A person outstretched for your help is the time to share your secret, not before. Loose lips exhaust mystery. How can knowledge lacking judgement ever get what's known? The penny drops *with* silence.

4. "Cease trying to grow. Whenever has a tree tried growing? It just grows knowing it will. As you branch into the life unknown, so too will you seed and sow. It all makes sense when you make sense. Crazy is sound when brains are found, but it takes one sane to play that game.

5. "I'm here to give more and taste it raw. A fresh serve to feed on from the seer's state and stage, and a throng of people who witness in wonder to wisdom, by learning to look and listen, to knowing the keynote to knowledge, serves thy Self through silence.

    "Let us pause for just that."

AWARENESS

With each passing hour, the crowd grew. Grassland lost in a sea of people settled and seated. As lunch passed, a seeker called out to Zenith, who was down below deck.

"Teacher, can you join us again, atop your craft and speak a little more; this time of Awareness?"

1. He met them just as before and said, "Awareness is the eye nature puts no lid on. All crossing its view impacts its own. No effect on its watch but to say of sight well-eyed shapes the matter at hand. How not when seen past and through?

2. "Worlds rise and they fall, but to picture it equal-measured captures life full-blown. As ocean hits land, so the sight of it meets contrast the same, on even terms. Each glance and look levelled by the view. Don't take my word for it. See for yourself. Here's a mirror to reflect on. Watch for wave after wave, the ocean it's on. Eyes as wide leave nothing from sight. From a ripple the slightest splash, to the surrounds all round; in its wake, what was is no more, and what is, is no less.

3. "Sight sees all being all. A clear view when clearly you. Even when not, you are, for clouds come and go but all along the sky remains. Here then I stand before you with no position from which to draw. For that which is, is all I am – an eyeful aware of its own.

4. "When eyes twinkle with what conveys, sight speaks. It's something to behold watching your words and ours. Tongues taking care more with how it's mouthed than to what we lip. Even words gone wild venerate when well said. If you must, shoot from the hip, but with real bullets. Firing blanks acts the part with little vision for the role. This scene casts true character playing the warrior's way. After all, it takes a sword to cut through dense matters. Slicing through expands the view. Open space when cutting straight and to the chase.

5. "Such room comes at a price. Who claims it seen pays the cost of a pair of eyes. Nothing seen is worth its weight short of treasure unseen. Come in blind and leave seeing. Here's an account of how a sharp eye cures stye: a warrior's armour sheaths when sand storms the desert. Skin-tight and tough. Wear made for loose stones. Now's not the time to succumb to the elements. Challenge the spectre of sand to scatter. We take hold riding the storm. Its grains milled and floured into the day as bright and blue.

6. "At times a grind breaking the habit of finding as found. Those adept break open any search stuck in a rut. Even the leaf lost from the tree *finds itself* on the

ground. Viewed that way sees life blow through as a wonder in the wind. Taking a leaf out of her book – Earth's story and how she speaks. She goes unheard, waffling words. Give it a rest and wake up to yourself. The writing's on the wall. *Eyes* read it, not mouths. Just a little quiet is all it takes. The silent serenade courts the rest. Tuned in and toned, the range voiced frames a picture that words can't. The outline tracks wisdom from a view that tells a thousand words. Keep watch or watch out.

7. "What else to see our errored ways? A hard look in the mirror faces it. I'll find no fault if you don't pick at it. Just bring to order cleaning your mess. A deep wash clears the excess and brings clarity. Suddenly, reflection mirrors an eye transfixing ours. Gazing upon gazing. Seeing its own into its own. Dual motion frozen in time. An eye-catching account of darkened night backing sunlight, or of light dressed in black, the ocean deep. Herein, all sees and sees all. Where the ocean cuts and waves, moves a soul supple enough to merge and emerge. It takes water to melt and fire to rise. Every drop steamed for good measure. Misted settings airing soul's mystery.

8. "In deep waters or to the stars, through this darkness and that, a place far and away draws the stare of a seeker most intense. Nothing escapes its gravity. The abyss swallows all. Such heavy terrain means there's no way out but through. Most fail the test, just as I did before I passed. Over that crossing, past the void in sight and stuff of dreams stands I, the widest eye."

AWAKENING

One of the priests said, "Today we rise and rest in ways just known. Bold enough to dream more with new eyes. Sick of driving round the bend and up the wall? Then lay your eyes upon a path most straight and watch the road open. Vision for the path and the one yet paved.

"Zenith, impart to us your view of the Awakening."

1. He said, "You who picks life surface-deep blindly weeds. But to shovel deep, vision unearths. From under the Earth and to the stars, power launches from working hands. Fuelled up from your thirst for living. How it's drunk, this cup of life shows your taste. And in the cup stirring, what comes to light tells a tale come true."

2. A rippled haze parted, giving way to waters deep and still. Eyes burning through it, he said, "Those risen bear their cross, tied to it in a show of strength. A firm stance plunging deep. Arms nailed open for that wide breath and look within. Seized today by the morrow's eye. A keen eye dressed well inside and out. Style sharpens the search, so why not? But those short on sight are straightened the hard way. Wacked between

the eyes for dozing off. Lost in sleep rings alarm bells but for the lazed who couldn't be bothered.

3. "Energy awakens a new day *and* way. Whatever your way and however it looks, the fog clears, getting the right rest. Focus comes and hits the ground running, transporting to even the furthest dream." A voice cried out, "But what to look for and how to see it?" Zenith said, "Look for a mirror and see into it. Seeing is the way and the way forward. God knows how!

4. "Eyes wide open captures the dream made just for you. Hold it aloft! May lightning strike down and course through. Anything to liven your heart to the beat of a different drum. Anything for you to just be You! Being equal *doesn't* mean the same. If it did, then whose garbage are you siding with? "Thunder claps a round of applause for shaking off the shit. Soul growth isn't pretty or easy on the eye. It stinks before it freshens. Digesting the smell, much like the scent, takes courage. I'm as vulnerable as you, and even more when it stinks to high heaven. After all, a spiritual ego cries foul more deeply than plain bravado. Turn a blind eye and the remains rot in hell. Shadows growing a mountain out of a molehill. Staring down the blind spot hurts the eyes. It means keeping watch around the clock. Nodding off won't do. Awake with no time to sleep. Awake: morning, noon and night.

5. "When dawn breaks, give time to smile, if only a grin within. At high noon, spend moments, if only a few, in awe of life. In the still of night, break from matter

riding galactic power, and lay to rest upon a bedspread of silence. Just like he who split the sea, may you wave your wand and scatter the stars. In the twinkling of an eye comes your dream in the making to wake to."

RICHNESS

An entrepreneur said, "Rich, am I, in money: self-made and owned. And for all of that, here I stand before you loaded with feeling that you are driving us to something unseen and yet known. What to say of the dollar saved and shared? All I can, amounts to this: business thrived through giving. People winning payment by way of merit. Acknowledgement inside and out builds success. Simple rules that work for your sake as much as mine. Trust placed in the keeper of funds went a long way. And now the urge to bank on something more. Seek, I do, for a different pay. A simple expense and bonus prize. For my soul to enrich I've heard the cost is me to deeply see. What am I to make of Richness here?"

1. Zenith said, "No amount of money can buy Soul. Soul is priceless. Lost souls are another matter. Therefore, lose in the way that wins. Check in when the chips are down. Tough calls are needed to invest upon. Then *your* soul is taken care of. Money or not, good or bad, the prize earned is a price paid. Never was it meant to be easy or hard, or just one or the other. Soul work is a whole trip driving the cost. Be sure to service its parts.

2. "Any fool can make a million, but those wise are one in a million. Health breeds their wealth. I'm talking a well-*being* with deep pockets to draw from. Their arms long as funding needs, and a smile as wide to stop the bleed. A little warmth goes a long way. Anything but a soul frozen in time. Cold hearts dampen success.

3. "Health and wealth come to those vibrant for it. Denying God denies money. Rather than say money is the root of all evil, evil roots for money lusting alone. No one to spoil the riches with. A deserted island! I'd much rather live on one. Anything for peace and quiet in a world mad for money. Friend yourself befriends money. The relation is born to fund and builds on interest. At this rate, all is welcomed. Trust once liable banks an asset. Money, although paper thin, spreads itself across a level playing field. Neither sporting more for one team or the other, money appears to those with skill and form. Any old team wins it, even the worst kind. But to win or lose unbeaten plays just and fair. An athletic attitude does just fine. Work it and it works for you. Laze no more in your laurels. Great comfort comes to those striving further than allows.

4. "Grow as a tree does. A tree knows growth is bestowed it. And have you ever seen branches of a tree meddle? Respecting each, scarcely they do. See the beauty of this and change everything. For Earth is proof enough of what money can't do."

CONTROL AND POWER

Politician's past and present stood, with one saying, "Instruct to us, Mr Speaker, a discourse on Control and Power."

1. Zenith said, "Your power's not your own. It sparks through from a source ever lit. It takes a brain to go with the current. Fooling around with power blows a fuse. The shock's on you!

2. "You've heard that power is in your hand. To this I'll add: energy powered courses through. Your every vein and artery feels it. But it doesn't stop with you. Let power run its course. Holding it explodes what it touches. In the same way what pumps a heart is blood aired by its source. Heart composed within a heart brings the bleeding under control. Severing these veins cuts the air we breathe. Sow self-control before it clots. Stifled knows nothing of proper restraint and neither you who bombs away. Now there's a heart attack waiting to happen.

3. "Those who play God purchase power through hard labour. Why waste time on business that costs your soul? Put your money away! What I'm selling can't be bought. Who am I to make power a brand? I'm not

your overlord or lord of control, and neither are you mine.

4. "God is greater than even His immanence. The greatest of the greatest is then a role. And in this service, what receives power gives to its source. A win for all uplifted. Remember, a stairway goes both ways. Up walking the same steps as down. Light a torch and shine above as you would below. Any power failure makes for a blackout – an absence of light in darkened night. No safe place to walk in this neck of the woods. Standing on others ensues. Feet stumble, for sure. Wait for the collapse, it's a given. The badlands soiled stand. Power in the wrong hands – from where loaded language lay.

5. "If not for the truth, all has no legs with which to stand. Cut straight and through, all talk sliced and diced. I make it business as usual, flying in the face of them riding against the wind. It serves a need to spread free from pinion rein through supple flights. Who are you to control where the wind blows? *Meet* it no matter the day, and things turn your way. A tempest has a temper and swirls a mess. You whose strength moves are powered more. Even if angry, remain true to it. That's the point, being with it. Truth feels all and at once. The truth of it *is* all and at once. Hand in hand the weak turn strong, from force to power. Dark suddenly light.

6. "In the ocean the storm's gift awaits one and all, through All and One. Now's no time to walk. The

dash to the shore may slash wrinkled feet. Never as happy as now to bleed O bleed. The sting of salt water toughens and heals. No time to wait. Nothing but life to lose, or so it seems. Move *your* way out of it. Much faith only a leap away. Still, eyeing vast depth is one thing, diving is another. And this kind makes no splash nor noise. A perfect display of power and control come silent and steady. Those as durable take the plunge, cutting deep and deeper still.

7. "The abyss draws the deepest dive yet. A descent knowing no way but through. Watch for passing terror when fear hits. Face it you die. Retreat and sharks eat. The former dies to live, the latter waits to die. No will-to-power waiting. Where the sun doesn't shine, the man of steel cracks it open. All kinds of muck flies. Wasteland's essence sells perfume that smells funny. It washes, swimming straight and to the gate. Then, past the rear end of nowhere, a beauty shines, potent and flooding. This submerged, power is all and control the same. All in this way *is* All, clear and complete. But a mistake to say All reigns or has the rule when such belongs to Thee, God Almighty."

BEAUTY

1. No room for pause as Zenith said, "Of Beauty, I say: These gardens and trees, the roads and lanes, the piles of dung – gorgeous! Every duck has a beauty all its own. Finding that asks to keep *your* own. To say this pleases and this doesn't is yours alone, for someone's beauty is another's beast. Life is beautiful: speaks three words too many. Why ruin the view, laden with words, when seeing says it all?

2. "Made up of forests and fields, let's walk the land a native to it. Human isn't just human. A bird isn't just a bird. We're Earth's story and song as told from one I to another. The breeze gives it airtime and broadcasts the tune over the clouds. Too, a weeping willow isn't just a tree. Her branches draped shows how arms hug. When the elements rage, how safe we are nestled under her care. Just as her trunk sustains the branches, so are we held upright by her strength to whether the storm. When nature settles, we thank the willow for the gift of coverage. Sometimes she needs more than a handshake; sometimes a hug and an ear, as sap talks its thousand stories. Would you cry as she does, and would you laugh the same?

3. "This walkthrough maps its own steps. Plans are made on the run. Just hold still long enough to envision it, the surrounds all around. A descent, even one with a running brook rests awhile. Boulders on the course make sure of it. Sometimes water stales, and sometimes the ride turns nasty and wild. When clouds cry, valleys feel it. Come what may, water is water however it streams. Likewise, you be you in whichever way. Nature's got you covered.

4. "Off across, distanced, lush terrain fronts a setting. Give all your nose to it. Aroma deepens when essence perfumes. Ride the mountain and your feelings as the climb peaks. Surfaced atop, know enlightenment has barely begun. A climb with mind behind also gathers it, resting here and moving there. This time the summit atop, mind rests silent and still. To speak of beauty wanes wisdom. And to hear from it, a perished pearl, echoes the pain of a gem once prized.

5. "Why wear clothes torn ugly when naked is best? Down with it, the nitty gritty loves muscling rough round the edges. Flex when pushed. Posing no threat smacks as less than wise. The man steps up, takes the hit, then dresses it down. After all, image is but a pointer pointed out. No arms throwing way, no pelvis thrusting movement. Nay, the real splendour is unseen in all things seen. What else must I say for you to make it with your Maker?

6. "To really shine, imbue your life. Life this way is best handled with both hands and by the scruff of

the neck. A touching gesture despite the face of it. Don't be fooled by her looks now. Peace missing turns things ugly. Clashing slides away and contrast pulls it close. Peace, its ease forms a magnet both sides wish to rub. A gap in the making bridged by life's own push and pull. The stretch across is narrow, and so is the gate. Any old walk won't do. You've got to be moved to walk through. Grace, the slightest touch, gifts it, in style and elegant.

7. "Now for the last step on the high ground of soul torn free from sight. The grab gestured the surrounds all around, taking one's breath. Airtime breaks the spell. It happened all in a moment's pause, wanting him and/or her. Desire creates the split, coming unasked as if it must. No-one came deciding, neither I nor you. But keeping watch saw it done, and without the faintest memory. Just like that, the last gap swallowed up by the splendour accounting for who I am."

THE DANCE

Stunned into full swing, the orchestra played. A different sound could be heard close and from afar. Rhythm spun a dance to its own beat. Many joined in the revolution. In the midst, a keynote smiled upon one such distanced on the bank's edge. At his greatest voice he said, "May you your voice, the way you speak, say a little more of this fine Dance."

1. Zenith said, "Intellect alone has two heads and two left feet. A paltry ration of rhythm each, flattened by patchy groundwork. Dead legs out of moves. Cemented in mud-thickened concrete. Brick-head! Stuck in the mind's game of building walls – four walls. In this prison, the jailer and the jailed are locked in for a smart reason. Bloody mind-talk! Chatter full of moves except the ones that count. And remember, how we step is judged all day, every day.

2. "It takes thrust to dance and moves galore to wipe the floor. To command the stage, contact the commander in charge. He hits the ground running, blending into the jungle on high alert. Commanding his troops takes focus on the forest as much as the trees. When it rages and fire flairs, it's time to find your feet. Walking your walk does so in step and in tune. One foot in front

of the other, forging ahead at any cost. No time to dance around the matter. The mire demands focus and courage to move silent and keep one's feet.

3. "Death breaking it down is better than apart. No point cutting the whole into parts. A piece still serves one whole slice. On the surface it looks the part. The bottom side tells the whole story. I won't lie, the pit has levels to it. One step then the next until a great fall. One breakthrough after another drives the process out of the mire. Progress marks the turning point. Great inroads are made where the river runs. Flow with it where it will, then settle aside where the sun burns beautiful, and sheen a polished routine. Shine by day rests assured at night."

4. "When wind gusts, time comes to leave the trees waving pleasure. There's also the time to cut it close, like moss over bark. We take on the world to shake it off. We march into this world and die out of it. The journey takes your best foot forward to cut it loose. In here, cosmic travel makes for a better home than a house. The build's no tall order. Just takes time to place it - the design tailored just for you. So, when lightning strikes and thunder sounds, stand again in the face of it. Summon the sky to how *you* stir. A little dance is all it takes for the heavens to open."

TEACHING

An intense shake of prayer rocked the embankment. Hands threw up in praise of God. Begging to Thee spread as if cut down from the knees.

Soon after, one such came forth shuffling fast her feet to the lip of land and water. The rush of her presence drew the people's eyes. She motioned to the teacher as though they were close. A moment's pause between each hushed the multitude. Breaking silence she said, "Old friend, tell of this Teaching you speak of."

1. And he said, "This voice is but a call to whet your appetite. It's hard to swallow without chewing on, so digest as much as you can. You choose the size being served. A good feed is mindful of greed. After all, gorged food doesn't sit well.

2. "These words are less about splashing and more about diving. This is no call to wave around prizing your entry. One way or the other, foam forms and then recedes. Water's still water, you just be You! Burst your own bubble before it pops.

3. "This rings true dialling within. It's a call touching on your need of me. You'll have it sorted when

breaking through the troubles of need. First reach out drawing in, receiving as much as is given. Help come true consults the owner, who grants the conduit their expertise all the while knowing each come to their own. Truth, a matter in the making. So let go of words, yours and others, except for the truth it holds.

4. "Nothing I say changes one's colours. Bland or vivid, you paint it. Be the mixer of your own dye. And stir well, blending colour when needed. Add to it another's substance if in you imparts you to. Whatever highlights your work of art. A clear view draws light, and colour adds shade. Tone and texture style the truth, but the brush with which I paint bares all.

5. "These teachings brush with death. Living on the edge has its own boundaries. A walking tightrope at times. Facing death ensues. But then dealing with death can take a lifetime's work. You may've died a few or a thousand times more, but I've died just once and woke up to the lie. Always knew it was suspect. Yet the evidence took years to compile. Enough saw charges laid on the grounds of impostering all that is with all that's not. Pride fights the charges and appeals, even unto death does its part. A little humility goes a long way. Pride speaks to none of it, saying 'It's hard to be humble when *this* perfect.' Who are you fooling? You're just a small part of all this said – no more or less. Yet your demands stake a claim no court will hear of.

6. "All this is owing to the student blowing power. Much is it said, 'When the student is ready, the teacher appears.' O the many who take the wrong turn with the wrong teacher. Right yourself, and the road taken turns out right. Ah, then there's the teacher whose trumpet blows all sounds selfless. All the while, hidden, their device plays to a more sinister note. Your secret's unsafe with you, let alone me. Light hides in no place, laying bare every space.

7. "The greatest teaching sources the greatest Self. Even then, the Self itself has its teacher. In the way the Almighty Lord is to the Immanent Lord, so human experience is to the human being a mentor too. If not, how else to be humble? Onto the next directive: the lesson today, beyond this very moment, teaches always and forever."

LOVE

Armi reached out, took the hand of her devoted one and said, "You who embodies life, speak to us its heart. What we call Love."

1. He said, "Why deprive your heart's need to bleed? Break it open to the comforts of affection. It's nothing less for love to sprinkle tears or a deluge. Privately, love is happy to rain more if so called. If love wills it, allow your clothes to sever, damaged skin and all. Deep hurt deepens the skin. It'll need to be thick to bear life and win. Must build yourself first, your very essence and freedom follows after. What good is love without freedom? What good is love lacking soul? Earning the dream of love and hard work go hand in hand. Nose to the grindstone. Love is counting on it!

2. "Getting to the heart's matter deals with fear, scraping the bottom of the barrel. If the well seems too deep and dark and all hope is lost, scrape a little more. Not in closure of the pit's process, but when fear closes in, open up to love. It takes reaching in the whole way to climb out and meet the day. It takes a love that's tough until it's not.

3. "For the hard of hearing, these words thus spoke speak at once. Who listens well, knows the heart's music strung close and from afar. Its song blows fire from deep within. A tune that speaks to swamping pain and to tears frozen in time of one distressed and bound to the loved one missing. Weaved also in strength and power, the restless and fragile find solace scaling high lands from a bottomless pit. Boring through mud and slime, nourishment came from the sounds underground. Vocals that speak of courage, yours and mine, in facing sadness torn. Whatever you bleed, if it runs through a hollow pipe, your heart beats clot free and pumps strong, stringing all veins to health.

4. "May well we weave akin ourselves, abandoned in bliss and then to peace. To surrender your will for thy fill, play this yearning song for the beauty of it. Its silence serenades the lover in you. Consumed by the quiet and consoled if split by it. A lover's reminder of devotion on fire. Heat pipelined to and from the source that sparked it all.

5. "Love is a mystery sustained when explained. When heart speaks, the allure remains. Love is such that strings of a heart pull, sever, and so mend. Love may even bomb the field of all you envisage. Still, love gone with, grows greater the field of freedom's play. So, if love cries out to you, heed her counsel to wherever she may take you. A nightingale circles the stars and rings a melody for one to catch its tune. Similarly, love calls too for nothing but her fellow self.

6. "Love's one hell of a ride to fly with. It'll take you up and down and all around. Just to board, waves will be made. How not when dealing with the ocean? Some will fish around surface-deep, blowing air and holding it. Other's use their gills to get around. And a few deepen it more for that wash throughout; all to where rich pearls muscle. It builds a strength that cracks the shell and breaks it open. Shining pearls well-earned. Now your health wears wealth and sticks to you like glue. Like any priceless gift, how it's used matters most. Experience knows the cost. When its wisdom sinks in, further and further still, the ocean deep and sun meet again exchanging stories of darkness and of light. And when it's all said and done, that is, when silence takes over and still waters follow, love's glory shall speak through every place hollow."

LIGHT AND DARK

Musicians abound playing; some in the sun, some in the shade. A backdrop of hands drum and shakers mix a beat. Cutting sounds from a wooden flute echo. And fingers plucking on strings of a harp keep a constant rhythm. These are classical times and more. Moved to speak, a voice called out saying, "Zenith, conduct to us, if you will, a whole piece on the Light and Dark."

1. He said, "Be present through dark terrain, in the night backing all things light. Shadows scorched to death by eye-glaring radiance. The stars above, they come to light, with heaven set in pitch-black. How things grow above the sky reveals the seeding beneath the Earth. When life springs forth it shoots from nowhere. Grassland around shows light as found, but it grows from the work in the dark.

2. "Light fills the space and Darkness empties it. Both work with each and sit well with each. If the sun and moon vanished, light goes on. Earth come or gone, voided space breathes life the same. If not, then why purge anything for which it is? A clean out makes room for light to peer through. Careful of what's turfed. Don't want to place emptiness above its value. That'll

void God, mistaking non-existence for existence. Darkness gone horribly wrong. No way of lightening up when shadows take hold.

3. "Reality: it's never just empty or just full. Our arms and legs walk all at once. Its contrast exists all at once. So, Darkness lays the canvas for Light to paint. The All is its art shaped into form. Form shaped from nothing less than a formless craft.

4. "Day isn't just light and night isn't just dark. A white night comes and saves a black day and a darkened light shows how. Shadow times cast into a different light. One that highlights beauty in the beast. All faults suddenly turn over a new leaf. Once weak now bumps strong. Strength drawn through a darkened resolve.

5. "Yet am I to meet any who could resist the dark after resisting it. And yet am I to meet any who could affirm the light after affirming it. Shadows don't shine but for the light in it shining, and light shines not without a shadow of support. Watch then for the night parading bright and for the day blinding sight. Light illusions end heavy and dark ones start evil. Look close to spot the lie. An honest account takes a long hard look. Getting real has brutal appeal. A brush with death helps. It drives the make-up artist to make up with art and mould a masterpiece.

6. "My art moulds armour that panther's suit. Its eyes power on through, stripping life to all of you. Its grace moves every mountain walked and its beauty

gives in layers. How much taken from each sighting is yours to sit with. Else I won't be spotted. If I was any more revealing, my*self* would spew out. In any case, I'll take self over ego. I can work well in low quality light and turn it around. But illusions are creepy; always trying to latch on at every turn. It's a battle beginning within and ends that way. My weapon of choice is the warrior's sword cutting a personage to the core.

7. "With ego replaced, shadows long cast reel back in. Now the dark bites in ways that catch on. Wounds laid bare come tended and wiped. Scars surface to such effect and leave a lasting impact. No excuse left but to face trauma and see eye to eye. After all, thy sword slices this story thin and weaves it thick. All things true piercing through. A dark parable reflecting Light in sharp detail.

8. "This is no fiction scripting light versus dark. Remember the Beginning? There was Darkness before Light and life thereafter. Darkness negating life only for Light to affirm it. Who would've thought voiding this or that means assenting This or That? So, the Dark of No-mind means the Light of Mind. One not without the other. Must I say it as easy as pie? This to throw the meat and potatoes in your lap: darkness beyond, lights up All within. Effulgence streaming through the hollow head of God.

9. "Fire melting every solid to liquid light. Pouring in and out, up and down, all around. Letting go with the

flow and with such a grip on life. No puzzles left to piece, paradox left to draw, or dualism left to fight. This is power's promise putting warfare to bed. All now between the sheets is a wrestle everyone wants. Ultimate touching as hands take hold. Abandoned in full to the gripping scene. A climax that comes to no end.

10. "And still full, beyond eyes rolled in bliss shone God's own across the grid. Stretching on and forever, the Self came silent over the field of play. No players or ego to bounce around with. The game-board's All That Is. Its pieces in place completes the puzzle. The part is as the whole itself, played at night purely for the light show. I'm talking a brilliant eye focussed straight ahead, taking all in and in stride. No thought for the moment come or gone. Just immersed like a child with a new toy playing.

11. "But to the one who feared *not being* versus *being*, then it happened: God as I deserted for what may never come to be. A daydream haunted by a nightmare running amok. Shadows awaiting the illusion bought as Real.

12. "Stranded and alone; bereft of God's green Earth and starlit space. More barren than the sea unplugged. Not even a speck of sand to rub with. Death well-known has nothing on never being. Try terror trembling through the worst of all deaths. The end itself! The final curtain – I am forever no more.

13. "Into the galaxy far and away, where no-one speaks and sees, I who individuates is thrust. Life or so it seems reduced to nothing. A walnut thrown into the biggest, blackest hole; a snowflake's descent into the desert; a volcanic display of harsh land and foreign climate. What erupts here has no echo, no sound – Nothingness.

14. "With nowhere to turn or go, witnessing can't bear to watch, but does. The fight is on! Knocked down and near out. To see stars, hope would glimmer. Never so paralysed as now. A desperate dance out of moves. Ego's last stand… I who boxed with no arms, no feet, no body, and with no-one, survived. Illusion alive for another day!

15. "This fool's fight hit for six. Lost who thought it won. Defence when surrender mattered. On the back foot when a step forward called. Small relief in opting out replaced by a lifetime of haunting. Loath to erase the greatest case of mistaken identity. A passion wrapped in existential crisis and existential fear. Seduced too by luscious lips smacking the perfect kiss, or so it thought. Concealed a lizard's tongue ready to catch its prey. Confusion over the frog with the prince. This story lives happily ever after in the prince of peace. But before then, even the conscious cosmos mistakes the eclipse of the sun as final. Core work needed else the sun burns out.

16. "To buy the Void sells the shadow. Its price steals light and costs you yours. Ownership in the wrong

hands yielding deadly results. A beautiful illusion, even one as impressive as the Void holds crushing trauma. It creeps up slowly and hammers down fast. Darkness to no end shining marvellous mimicries. The pit, we know it plays by other rules: spitting fire while keeping us warm; spewing lava while cooling us down. And so does the Void in its own way. All to mould us to it, carving stone-dead silence."

ENLIGHTENMENT

1. Zenith continued, "But for the life of Light, enlightenment equals a close encounter. The experience alone contacts an alien world suddenly known as one's own home. Even so, the greetings exchanged will fail to Light, but for when your good days and bad turn perfect. And when they do, take heed, for a change will sweep over and turn the day dull short of One life through one's life. What then of life less than Light? Just more ego in the way to live with.

2. "It takes One and All to clear all parts, and it takes the Absolute to Light One and All. If these words less than sparked from life's own ark, they'd come diluted and flood in a sea of water. Who thinks I say what I say and write what I write, think again. For wisdom is God's as spoken and as written. Who but God lights these words and darkens them?

3. "The Light's own lightness means that via All and That, and the Lord's lordship means just the same. So, a trees tree-ness means what it is and is what it means. A tree is a tree is a tree in every way. And any leaf from any tree, varied or not, is still a leaf, still itself. In

the same way, Self is just itself and the I is just I, and the Self *is* I. Nothing of I is birthed except its death. I'm no different than you even when sliced that way. Cut it anyway you like, here's the story in full, of the miracle and the magician...

4. "...All fell silent, without sound. In every place a spotless sky dressed in black. Space on leave with time. Replaced by infinite space and time. No pointers left to give or take. Front back and sides woven the same as up, down, and around. The eye that took no form in eyeing itself. Not even a witness to come forth and take the stand. If there's a thought to rise with, here now won't stand for it. All that carries this state just knows it knows. Self-contained with no vessel to speak of."

5. "Struck still before it all began. The origin of it – *All*. Into the cosmos the Eye eyed. My, God is God. Known, thus knowable. All alive as if jumping. Creation dancing divine madness on a trampoline backdrop. Silence pulsates as the soundless source composes the perfect score.

6. "Then, taken aback, the eye is shown. Lucifer flings a line of bait made for hooking. Sinkers cast a heavy weight. And though the temptation spoke just like that, at the click of the fingers, its offer lingers, taking forever to finish. Be sure to leave alone its lure. The master of illusion entangles with an array of tricks, pitting himself against the Lord's Self. Throwing down what you're not, up against all you are. To the

eye that sees, Lucifer said, 'All this, the entire world, its power is yours to have and to hold. Liable are you no more to nothing and no one. Take it now and my hand, and I alone will raise you up, over and beyond.'

7. "All temptation twists in a knot. As slow as the eye is shown, deny him fast the throne. Why lord deluded over the All? No good comes from claiming yourself as the law of the land. It's well enough being a boss without being bossy.

8. "He who watched was thrust forward, then came to a stop. He saw loving darkness setting the scene for the story told by the knowing Self seeing itself as Itself. No more than oneself nor less than that. Great presence arose. Awareness amazed and awed – the fearless kind. An eye without moves couldn't move. Nothing more to let go. Just surrender itself! No extras. No ties. Nothing affixed. What came went. A non-event in the making. Just as the ocean waves into the shore, so the flow of one state to another arose.

9. "Suddenly, power stood fierce and mighty tall. With a roar that rumbled and a quake that shook, all transfixed on the wave rushing forth. Strange and wondrous, the cripple freed up and set itself for impact. Embraced for the clash of an eye for an eye. I *as* Eye soared tsunami high. Like eyes rolling Shakti pleasure, impact climaxed a thousand times more. Blinded by the night and by the biggest bang. Intense and intimate. God's passion coming all over.

My God! My God! My…"

NOTHINGNESS AND ALLNESS

Silence settled upon the people.

Then, upon the outskirts of the embanked hill, a solitary figure emerged. Her clothes worn and hair entangled, she looked foreign to the people and the land. An outsider passing through, exuding unusual beauty and a powered bearing. Little by little she came forth. A thought-provoking presence for them cut nice and neat. Suddenly her walk that so glided halted still. Just enough to be heard much and seen little. And she spoke, her voice travelled saying, "Long have I sought to solve it like you and speak on all accounts. Your voice given has struck a chord, and still I'm caught between verses – *I am* verses *I am not*. All which battles and duals with life, fighting to death and grappling survival. And here you stand in the truth of it, beyond and free.

"I too have come to nothing and to it all. Down and collapsed and up and risen as if built that way. Frozen and frigid of the terror beneath, only to ride the tsunami's every drop. Nothingness came again erupting under the wave of Allness. Yet you say the Void spits love and swallow's death. I ask, am I ingesting it all within, or am I denying the stomach its fill? Food that settles it once and for all. For years I've felt off, and only now this very day have my insides so turned that I must vomit. Please, would you speak more of this mountain and its summit – the Nothingness and Allness?"

1. Zenith said, "The Void! Picture this: an astronaut stranded in deep space with no support of crew and ship. No contact at all. All planets and stars fallen from the heavens. The universe stripped of anything and everything. Its power shaken until nothing remains. No-thing mistaken for what cannot be!

2. "The world no more and all in it. The whole body cut away and thrown into the fire. Decayed and dissolved is just the start. Wait till the end itself! No mind left to think or way to process. Even the witness stands no more. Laid down by its predecessor on watch. Just as suddenly I came blindfolded, hijacking the moment, and saw it *this* way: the entire script torn to shreds. No actor present or story with lines let alone a movie to script and film. The coming attraction's just hypnotic viewing screening emptiness.

3. "Viewing it travels into it. The flight across gives rise to terror. A bomb dropped nuclear warfare. Only it's *me* left to wipe out. All too alone. Never more so until the Void swallows me whole. Agony cut short and sharp, as if shrapnel pierced the very core. Killing me, and for good – that I may never again come to be. But by then the thrust from the explosion has its own push. Propelled beyond what I am versus am not.

4. "The very fabric of I splitting-apart at the seams. Crumbling into the field where nothing and no one lives. It's a strange view eyeing the Void as the ride pulls over the cosmos to death made final. The journey where silent screaming falls on deaf ears. A

slow slaughter and trip across to what is no more in sight – past the crossing of the Rubicon, the point of no return. The last flickers of light fading fast. Such life force blazing like a shooting star reduced to this, a pebble. Scorched to impending death worse than burning flesh. Extinguished to extinction; to bear it more, *this* I could no more.

5. "Don't do what that I did, kick and scream with no legs and mouth to show for it. Caught in the final apocalypse with no stomach for it. 'Tis a hard punch to take fighting paralysis with no arms. Just too afraid to stand with the rarest, staring down the Void. But to turn from it is worse than staring down the barrel.

6. "There's a reason we're drawn into the desert of hunger and thirst. On the other side the field of dreams come true. From death-valley, the worst of all fear, to the mountain peak, the best of life here. Go with the wind no matter the condition. The flight into the Void will crash and burn. No survivors except what sees death itself. What sees the disaster unfold remains unseen. But, to be as such bears the brunt of death and lives to tell the story. The story that carries on with all momentum. Suddenly, out from the ashes the phoenix rises. The breadth of wing opens to the sun's light for its flight. It took faith spread far and wide over fear inside. Courage to walk the line through the fire. The first step may be your last. At that crossing, the end itself, Nothingness gives way as God steps in.

7. "Allness! Picture this: an astronaut at home in deep space with full support of crew and ship. Close contact on deck all the time, and in every place. The source of all planets and stars resetting the heavens. Cosmic power retrieved back from the land of the dead. The universe clothed in anything and everything. Today, fashioned in clear black. No content left to colour it with. Context draws it and frames all over in plain sight.

8. "All perfectly itself. Life preceding form took to the field *as* it. Connection complete – All-presence ticked as here right now. No head or body count needed. One represents All and All represents One. The power source is fully charged. Up and running, Vegas lights dim by comparison. We know when a city blows a fuse, darkness abounds. How happy are we when its power returns? When it lights up, so do we. What if the whole universe did just that and at once? Black night expressed as God's light. Radiance from which all is known.

9. "Knowing the world is one thing, the knowing All is everything. In the way that a human being knows, so a dog knows in a dog way just the same. Of its dog-ness nothing is left to know or to grasp, for a dog is a dog is a dog. Its very dog-ness is what is meant. It being what it is, is what knows what it knows. All as Known and the Known as All virtue of the dog being a dog.

10. "The All jumps alive standing still. We feel it through a feather's brush and child's loving touch. We see it in

a friend's smile and when going the extra mile. The eyes have it. See into mine if you wish for All come Known. Let's breed a little peace, or a lot, and rock deepest space with its dance on our face.

11. "And then it happened as if it must. A gate guarded by the crawling keepers. No key pass accessed for the powers professing power. Just for those who hold it without claim. Lucifer, you sneaky snake! But first, imagine the field of the All as a dance floor, and the Glory of God revealed just one dance. And in that instant the whole field lit up, alive, as God unmoved busted a move. Elegance so stunning and silent, far-reaching and stilled, reflecting the dance itself. No DJ mixing a beat or production crew creating a scene. This is no place for a director choreographing the stage. No one exists behind the scene, let alone any actors on it. What this is, is *being this*. No hidden composers or staged show. No lights, camera, action and boom here's God – no! All was just of its own, starkly bright and stunningly obvious.

12. "Now picture being taken from this. Cut from the greatest orgasm. Having the rug pulled from beneath and thrown back to where the cosmos opened. The magician's hand presenting an offer for the taking. Draped through no thought, temptation spoke a message known by just how it's known. And Lucifer said, 'Having reached over the sky and stars you now stand beyond all climatic account. Free to be and do as willed. All this the entire world, yours for the taking if you so choose. Take it and my hand so that we may

be wed.' Privy to the All and aware of its fill, the eye saw the food as bait. Greed absent of the Creator's creed. And in a blink, I let it go. For Eye am All and All is Eye. All as Eye is All. And in a flash, that which keeps the gate, marshalled no more.

13. "Transport came. The ride that pulls away went right back from whence it came. O, dear Allness, bearing witness to it stupefies. Divine dumbness held statue still in such a gaze. God-struck beyond the eight points of speech. Pressing to move the Force that won't and then no care as great *to* move. When so rested in the love and peace of one's home, all is full. Nothing more left to rent. This house is off the market. Sold to what made you a steward of it. Its price costs you your life, only to resurrect it upon land come true. Stunned by the beauty of the milieu, the setting stands tall and homes all for as far as eyes see. A real-estate success reaped beyond reach and grasp. Power alight in one's palmed hand. Seeing all it holds and how it unfolds. All things God in the land of the rising Son."

SALVATION AND ENLIGHTENMENT

And one who saw through the crack of the cosmos past the end in sight said, "It's said you're a man on hand with a new set of tools. Here among us to hammer hardened ground and build within from waters deep.

"What you impart cuts complexity and shares it simply. Wise words destined to boom, across all sea and sand and mountain tops and land. All things coming to God has come as all things God. In what knows-how we put our trust. An ear on the unsaid even more than said.

"Today, down under, the secrets of the deep burst open, surging skyward and most high. Where truth levels all types, you stand apart as others assort. You came true, a face of faith itself. In you I see the Lord coming, blazing great glory across the world. It's known also that your footprints of days be gone did gather you dust. Now your feet lands and leaves its mark. Your imprint we'll save for the next foot standing ground. Our gift from you presenting a hardware of health. The full kit on display upon a river flowing into folklore. From one bank to the next, may your God and ours build for us a bridge between Salvation and Enlightenment."

1. And before more, Zenith said, "This poem saves as much as enlightens. The same sun shining for many

skies. An original lens to view from and one eye just for such purpose. Our greatest telescope yet.

2. I'm here for the salvation of Man and for Man's leading Light. Come my way if armed for war and ready for death. When death comes and the All leaves you gobsmacked, your day of conflict will rise again until mastery come full – until top becomes bottom. "God help those on high wronging low, for enlightenment like salvation is born from the bottom up.

3. "Christ wants you naked as Buddha, and Buddha wants you dressed for Christ. Buddha sits in the darkness beyond and Christ lights it within. Too long has the monk's scalp had hairs on it. Begging practiced by a soul needing saving. And too long has the one saved and brave declined the lights splendour invite.

4. "I've saved a story that needed saving. One that goes early and arrives late. Off topic like the poem it is, weaving in and out until the end clears it. Building from scratch, start constructing down the middle and assess the elements in contrast. On one side all that limits can empower too, and on the other side all that frees can just as inhibit. Choice weaves a fine thread. We either sew well or poorly. Needling between heaven and hell pays for it in limbo. The truth is we're here in heaven or its absence, stitching ourselves in truth or not in truth.

5. "The staircase from Earth to Heaven is steep. Each step purifies or can just as punish. Purgatory works like that. Tripping up and slipping down calls for a

sense of humour. Using it builds the right amount of traction. But beware, since enlightenment too has its own oil slick. Hard to see when the colour looks clear. Grease all over when attitude slithers. Hard enough to climb or descend and now a nest of snakes to combat a bad fall. And demons below, bottomed, in wait for the worst collapse. The helpless must find help, must choose help. God knows our choice – who is Thine. Released safely, a cure expels your poison.

6. "For ye wafting Satan's stench, its gas blows deadly silent. Its fate all too dark to explain in detail. Wait for the explosion around the corner. Do the shadow work and you'll catch it at full force beating its own with a bat. Assault and battery inflicting a strangle hold until the beast is beaten. Doing so means fighting in dark terrain with the lights on. Nothing I can say about life in the dark when blind to it. Avoid that like you would the plague.

7. "Soon enough, all souls of the shadow need God's rescue. Help yourselves before salvation must. Purge the putrid from Pluto's pit. No other way to climb out of such a rut. And when set loose, least forget your freedom saved enlightens the way.

8. "The structure that saves is upping its plan to spread the foundation and build upon its blocks. A fortress long-solidified is bridging all to higher ground. You've taken stock and built over the river narrow. Now cross the gap your soul forgot to fill. Muse little on how to cross. 'Tis no time to dwell. Streaming thought floods

the current with rips. Ego wants the struggle. It loves to be saved, crying, 'More, give *me* more.' Christ wants your next step. It's indeed a threshold to cross. One that ends death by drowning. And for this a bridge is built to carry forth and sink the ego's stand.

9. "Jesus steers within for you to go there. In there and out here his coming has come. Now his hand gestures over and beyond. No chance left when the time arrives. Either die for the truth marching forward or pick up where your life lain. Truth pulls all paths ahead. First look deep – within. No matter the motion, stay the course rocking your core. It sounds rough, but I tell you, the word contained travels back from whence it came. It ships aboard with all ears docked for loading and sails abroad over all seas serving all needs. Its voice carries and echoes down through the ages. Self-named too through I and you. Sovereign and royal. No different to the Lord in this day and that."

THE CHRIST

Across the embankment, murmur muttered. The people began to speak amongst each and all. Silent settings gave way to a growing noise. Before long the haste of it spilled over. Troubled and enraged, insults flew. A scene barking outrage at the voice saying what God speaks. In light of this, some elders came forth calling for calm.

Tempered somewhat, rage simmered under the skin. Amongst it all a priest gave voice for those upset. To Zenith he said, "Who are you to speak of such a thing? We know when night brings the end of day. And here now you say thee, our Lord, dwells again with us: the Son formed from the formless Father."

1. Touched by truth, others rallied for Zenith. As wind sweeps over a forest, support spread. A large sway over trees unmoved. The silent few grew legs and marched a major beat, stomping the lie. One voice silenced the many as Zenith said, "The settled and seated among you drives yourself the way home. If you who struggle to be as stilled, how then to place the seat of rest let alone its throne?

2. "Whoever comes today for more than a moments rest, lend to me your ears. For what fills all moments in all times is here now brimmed over. Vision pouring out

and raining down for the seer to soak and bathe in, and a mouthpiece for God's wisdom reaching every corner of the Earth. The voice through which the Son's word speaks has spoken much. And while you hear it from this mouth, the speaking of it is too an ear full. Christ here right now unfolds his own flesh living. God's descent diversifies using one's own for Thee. Like the tree that grows, the seed lives in all its branches and as much as the root itself.

3. It takes a panther's eye and ninja's foot to catch God's walk moving this talk. If through Thee all things are possible, then move as silent and be as still for the Word thus spoken to speak in you. Why must we stamp up and down for his foot alone imprinting the land? For our foot marks as good and greater too when placed by God who lands it. What looks one foot at a time is both at once painting turf in the body's style. *This* painter forms a close brush with death, painting for Jesus and signing off unknown. If this weren't so, if my name remained, however could Jesus save art, or Christ enlighten it?

4. "Are you, any of you so blind to the artist bearing no name? I come silent so Christ can speak. Whenever has God's own sketched art that wasn't picture-perfect? Man's own making is for whose piece scribbles. Art lost in a world of fart and writings too in a wordy book. Or we read it wrong, closing the right book and on others. And we call ourselves Christians.

5. "You who see the flower cut from the garden hold in you a thorn. Remove it before all colours bright

fade. No single soul exists. If it did it does only to be as saved. Saved by One more than one. Every flower and all amongst it are more than that. Gods, I say! A garden full of God *as* God.

6. "The master chooses the friend now, just as when he did then. And friends you may be in ways yet known, since now is your proof to be yourself all things hallowed. But to you made rotten your fruit grows foul. I warn you and all you: all tomatoes thrown my way will turn your blood bleeding for Christ. Turn away this pain you suffer it.

7. "High upon this bridge I've stood, an eye stands perched. Sight on watch for missiles and bombs. Waging war on this landmark detonates before this. This body stands the test of time, and the test of the one who blew it. Its pathway across is narrow and has backing throughout. It's steeled within and endures without. On one side a pillar cemented by Jesus the Son of man and the other by Christ the Son of God. Comfort on both sides for the trek across. Footing saved for a demanding walk. The journey from salvation to enlightenment and beyond.

8. "Water under the bridge has passed. Religious and spiritual meet united to that merging both. Christ-Conscious and Buddha's Body – the gatekeeping of Mind and no mind at all. Some call this state the Self, and it's true I am That. It's a field also, a screen of sorts where the standards are set for ultimate viewing. No amount of will changes God's. Realized or not, God's Will Is and you just Are.

9. "First, just come as you are and knock on the door. Intend for the kingdom come. Even you locked out year after year, the first step is to prune its gardens and mow the lawns. Work at it enough and an invite comes. A key, yours, cut for a tall palace where faith and trust open the greatest good. Come *in*. Your own staircase pristine and white stretching onwards and up. Stairs that climb all over the serpents rise. Each flight sealed door tight holding the sight of blinding light. Nothing misplaced in such a place. The setting's all-inclusive and dines with the finest sign. Waiters serving only the best. Each chef a disciple of food's own essence. All no less than thoroughly filled.

10. "In the main room, Rembrandt's walled across and Buddha's seated with it. Tao art fills the space and Zen carved in stone makes it home. The pantheon faith lights the place and all in it. Krishna's flute sets the ambiance. Zoroaster's deeds live on, supplying wood for the fire and Muhammad's spirit stokes it. All settled into more than one's name and one's rank. All redefined by the greatest sign. Unearthed by the Lord's death and re-birth. God's avatars basking at once in the warmth of the Son's heat. The legacy of God in Christ himself from one age to the next; Aquarius forth.

11. "All is as it is, just as I is as I is. Even as you are, an invite asks for more - the best of All. To be so, your choice walks the future straight down the line. From one door to the next leaves the aroma of those who

came before. Mysteries of the great ones aired and shared. And then, fragrance by Jesus for all who trace the trail. Perfume of stirring sense and alluring scent drawing a great nose to a greater view.

12. "No standard rooms left in this part of the cosmos and nothing that can be bought. God owns it all and shares it freely. First, the superior room providing luxury for first-class dwellers. Next, the deluxe room meeting every need to plant the seed. Then, the grand room laid out with all and everything in it. And lastly, the supreme room with the flawless floor and roofless top. It homes Christ's own view of all that, his ascent and descent."

THE END

Embittered by the word come spoken, the old men in skirts scrambled for their Catholic caps, blown off by the winds of change. Christian's hell bent on heaven were first to walk, mouthing this and that as they stomped off. Next followed the procession driving love and light, praying for Zenith and those homed in the pit down under. Curiously, the monks pressed forward and leaned in. Even a Hindu emerged, as did a Mohammedan and a Zoroastrian. All clothed in devoted apparel coming closer to each. All wise to the thin disguise. Drawn in by a common sense on the same grounds.

As one procession left, another arrived. Along the Boulevard, those on bikes dressed dark in leather sat seated on their beasts. One member nodded to the other members. At once they parked then walked the bank, past the people making way and came to a stop at its edge.

With eyes set upon Zenith, their leader said, "We've heard about your ride, the craft you use. It's said you drive it freely, risking life and limb. A law unto your-Self. Are you so the outlaw they say you are?" Before more was said, sirens coloured red and blue deafened ears. Police on patrol, a large squad, braked hard their prowlers behind the beasts, blocking the road and any way through.

Tension grew, and with it, fear. Armi could feel it shudder through Zenith, who took it in and poured it out. Fearful of chaos gone mad, sweat arched his brow. A perceptive eye could see it, great instincts could taste it. Armi stood at Zenith's side squeezing gently his hand with hers. And with that she looked at him, a stolen glance. Eyes that met. Hers that levelled his. Strength grew, enough to make the fear his own.

Police power spread, cautioning off the crowded space. In single file the unit moved in on the hunt, heading straight for the gang and Zenith in sight. Zenith raised his hand to draw their focus.

At that moment, the leading officer spoke strongly to him and with force. "We were called in to bring order to a disturbance of your making. You who walks with all forms of life, what's your business with these angels and rebels? Bring your craft here and with all forms of ID."

Zenith said, "First, keep the rubber bullets in your guns this time. Shooting at peaceful protesters, your own people. And no public apology for it. Hasn't your Chief Commissioner disgraced himself enough? Next, my business with them is not yours. I'll show you myself, every bit of ID. I'm coming to you! Just a moment or two to answer your question with theirs; you'll see governance beyond your own and ordered law in chaos. And when so, you'll still draw your guns and shoot. The Government's arm, after all. But I tell you, your guns are shot and your bullets are limp. My way stares back at yours. A gaze that freezes to death. A killing like no other. Life in review coming to you and a passageway through to light radiant at the end of the tunnel. I'm there the other side, if you dare."

"Then if you dare, tell us who you are," yelled a voice from the crowd.

Zenith said, "I already have for those with ears. If I've blasphemed, set your cuffs around my hands. If not, if truth stands to reason, the people will sit with these words and watch the setting sun. And you, you facing I, will stand at ease and ride off into the sunset and I'll raise my hand aloft."

The golden hour blazed across the sky and so with it his words. Peace settled upon the people. Freedom shook off the shackles. Such release brought many to tears. Some grew loud with laughter. A few dared to let loose splashing all colours about. Plenty moved and grooved, while others lay still. All a symbol of their own dance. Armi motioned to Zenith to pull up anchor. Then she switched a setting, sparking power. From the river's bed, water sparkled and shone. Melbourne's heart appeared healed and pollutant-free.

The craft drifted with the tide. And with that a roar came, sounding out from voice over voice, "More, more, speak to us some more."

Zenith looked to the sky then down within. 'Twas a lasting pause that drew great silence. Suddenly his eyes locked upon the throng, and he said, "Just as I'm with Melbourne and so with you, so are you with I beyond just me. As have you listened to this speech, so have I. Neither soak into me nor this speaking, but do listen, finding out to what is said. Feel the truth and what to stomach, touching base with instinct. Eat just enough to please right. Else too little remains hungry, and too much bloats hurt. Thoughts alone undernourish and overfeed, breeding scarce supplies or a gluttonous punishment. Mind-pains close in horsing around with thought. Cut loose! Why trot reigned in? You are free, free I say, to gallop unfettered in wonders wild. Move like the wind, fast or slow, whatever the flow. Seasoned traveller's use patience. If over patient then a fast mind helps. Ride it home – from where dreams come and to where they come true.

THE END

"A dream home takes time to build. The day that comes when home is yours, castle strong, no shore abutting ocean runs it aground. How when where lived spans more than the seven seas? My home cradles Earth in one's own hand. Here the expanse is great and the planet small. Hardly a thought to hold and barely a mind to wash with. When that time comes, the next step climbs to the mind aware from the mind no more. When so, the tide on thirsty sand will speak for the ocean deep. The seasons will show their state, on land and in water. To thrive with the elements, here's the forecast: the setting shows great warmth and clears all clouds. Down under, a whale's song and dolphin's laughter echo the ocean's joy. Happiness fans the air and peace is cool about it. No words left in its wake. Why describe the perfect sunset when it's best to watch? If I am to say what it is, it wouldn't be. Leave it unsaid for silence instead. Just an eye on the sky for spirit to fly.

"Glory be to the Lord O Thee as you, Melbourne's own, hearken to this speech. For now, in marriage paper-free, the next dream calls to Armi and me. After a light float upon the ocean, I may return." Words leaved and space breathed. Dusk came and fell to the ground.

With shouting whispers, Zenith raised aloft his hand saying, "We our city stands again. Filth has fallen under my heel and yours. Drive it in and all the way home. With our feet firmly planted, and on the throat, the leader of this world is bound to choke. At every turn, the chosen is you who press on. Just to give all is all to ask. As I steer into the loving dark, rage festive and right to passion's work by day and by night. For the time that comes is already here to snap back to it and *wake up, wake up, wake up.*"

AFTERWORD

Writing this book first commenced early in 2001, and was initially meant to be a book about love. Later that year, the experience of 'Enlightenment as Allness' versus Nothingness occurred. Life as it was previously known was no more, and so was the book.

The book was self-published (not to the public) in 2003. Soon after, it became obvious that it wasn't the right time to become an author. Spiritual inexperience and a lack of life know-how were all too evident. Moving forward, the intention was to fully integrate the experienced Enlightenment in order to become One with what it is as a way of life. To help this process, another book was written (from 2004-07) and self-published (again, not to the public). While consciousness was elevated to a desired capacity, the efforts over the preceding six years had taken its toll. It was as if the human body needed time to adapt to holding within it very high states of consciousness energy. Time wasn't given to rest and recover, which in turn had a cumulative effect on the body. Rest and recovery became the overriding priority over pushing oneself onto the world's stage. This also gave the opportunity to confront the personal unconscious. Reintegrating the self and retrieving the soul in full were sought. This precipitated a dark period of my life that lasted for nearly four years. During this time, some poor choices were made. Enlightenment was lost in an instant. Due to a hedonist lifestyle, demons were invited in and eventually possessed the body. A saviour was required to transcend out of the negativity of the ego. Physical death felt imminent and guaranteed, if not for the energetic clearing (exorcism) and salvation of Christ. Thank you, Lord Jesus, for your salvation.

After the initial shock of the possession, it's clear that it did, in no small part, occur because they the demonic forces knew the threat posed to them if the author's soul was with God. Walking out of the darkness and into its trauma, I began writing *this* book again as therapy after a 10-year hiatus.

Zenith and Armi can be viewed as one character or separate. Zenith has his own connection with the man upstairs. That said, he first identifies himself as Christian the moment he says, "And we call ourselves *Christian*" in *The Christ* poem. It's as if Zenith's teachings prior to that earned the legacy left by Christ the Lord.

It's left to the reader to assess themselves the book's themes of dream versus reality. The ending, *"wake up, wake up, wake up,"* may imply that the throng are dreaming, or that Zenith is simply saying the words as wisdom. Or maybe the *dream setting* isn't that at all. It could be everyday reality, and then Zenith's *vision* 'til the end. Or, could the entire parable have occurred within a dream?

Zenith, like its word-meaning (apex of success), is the culmination of the human consciousness condition. To reach that, to become that which you ultimately are, experiences the Word of God as He comes and as He is.

It's most interesting that the parable is set in Melbourne. This alone gave me the opportunity to highlight the themes of authoritarian rule, mass compliance, and civil unrest that gripped the city (and indeed the world) during 2021-22.

Rewritten from start to finish at least five times, (the last time from April 2020-July 2021) the parable has also had hundreds of book titles. Months on end would be spent contemplating one title after another. Eventually, on July 14th and 18th 2023, both the main title and subtitle emerged as that. By the end of July 2021, 17 of 29 poems were fully recitable. This venture abruptly ended when my 65-year-old mother became one of *many* who've died suddenly after being administered the Covid *vaccine*. Hospitalized within two days, suddenly turned to palliative care, and death on day 9. A brave and fierce stance was then taken against the totalitarian agenda of the unconstitutional, unethical (breaking the Nuremberg Code's principles) state government, and compliant employers for coercing human beings to effectively become lab rats for the Elites who centralise power and control over the masses (i.e. vaccine mandates/passports). Lately (Aug 2023), I've begun rememorising a few of the poems and will continue to evolve this in order to perform them for an audio book of *City Prophet*.

Zenith is all soul. His embodied Self resonates strongly with the symbolism of the planet Pluto and Darkness of Shiva. Certainly, the plutonian energy forced its way into the writing process and demanded that Zenith be at One with Godhead's Unmanifest/Nothingness for the Power of God to manifest. Having choice ripped away by force brought the soul to its wound, and took from the self-identity a sense of power. One had to work through exactly that to earn power back, stronger than before. Surrendering, I went along for the ride. Then there's the wound that's always open, for poison to seep out and medicine to pour in. Our greatest gift the elixir and our cross to bear from life to life. Working with both wounds, as different as they are, ultimately serves the transmutative process of Creation into evolution.

AFTERWORD

Finally, the discipline of enlightenment seems not for everyone. Its way radically and periodically removes the recipient from the world. Rejoining the world as a Mystic may or may not happen. Much depends on one's ability or lack thereof to communicate the reality of Self. It's much easier to remain silent, and understandably so. Speaking or writing of such a reality is absorbing and consuming. For the Mystic, it's the most difficult of endeavours, until it's not.

Following self-realization, a contemplative approach to life ensues and is that way due to the intense need to embody the initial experience of enlightenment and then evolve beyond it. One might ask why this process of embodiment can and does take so long. I'll say this: imagine finding yourself suddenly perched on top of the tallest mountain. So tall that it reaches into outer space, revealing the entire universe and a glimpse of its greatest revelations. And then, just as suddenly, the experience is taken from you. You're back grounded on Earth at the bottom of the mountain – forever changed by the view of the summit and forever longing to re-experience the sense of homeliness that comes with it, inclusive of the paradoxical Void of loneliness. Only this time one must walk up the mountain to uncover God's seeming secrets. It's this paradox (of existence versus non-existence) which drives the recipient all the way up the mountain. It will take time to climb to the top, step by step. Not everyone makes it... the Void is crushing. There are those who do, the small minority still – those Mystics who survive after the final apocalypse.

Be alert, your time may come at any time. The inception of this author's experience occurred while becoming lucid in a dream. A loud *inner pop* was heard that immediately altered the perspective into a transformational shift: transporting the awareness into an acceleration of inner awareness, aware of the timeless spaciousness of the all-encompassing non-formative blackness filled with the omnipresence, omniscient and omnipotent quality/ character of God, better known as Allness. When your time arrives, you'll remember that the flight into the Void will crash and burn. Courage is with you to walk the line through the fire. At that crossing, the end itself, the Nothingness of the Void gives way as God's Allness steps in.

AUTHOR'S BIO

Daniel Orr, in his role of the Mystic, has for the past 22-years worked in complete solitude, removed from the world in order to bring it an account of his experience thus gained. The result is *City Prophet*: a book that transports the reader and breaks new ground. With wisdom rich in imagery and grounded in nature, the parable breathes fragrance and fire, confronting the world and explaining to it the essence of reality in all its enlightenment. He says, "It's taken this long to complete as there is no more difficult task for the Mystic than to explain what is in essence unexplainable."

Daniel's passion extends to performing the parable and its inherent poems for an audience. He lives in Melbourne, Australia and is currently working on his next book, *Street Prophet: Standing on a Stool*.

www.ingramcontent.com/pod-product-compliance
Lightning Source LLC
Chambersburg PA
CBHW072013290426
44109CB00018B/2229